ELIZABETH

ELIZABETH

ANONYMOUS

GROVE PRESS, INC., NEW YORK

First Black Cat Edition 1984
ISBN: 0-394-62037-2
Library of Congress Catalog Card Number: 83-83038

Printed in the United States of America

GROVE PRESS, Inc., 196 West Houston Street,
New York, N.Y. 10014

85 86 87 5 4 3

ELIZABETH

CHAPTER
one

There is dust on the sill—the specks like myriad people seen as from a mountain top. Were there no breeze nor the passing of a servant's hand, would the sunlight move it by such slow degrees as one can never notice? Perhaps I might seal the room in order to discover this, but life does not permit such foibles. Agnes would question the closing of the study. Wives are ever curious about such things. Servants would ask me humbly for the key. Glances would be exchanged behind my back. I would be at a loss to explain my actions. Even now I appear to be explaining to myself my hesitation in such matters.

You move about your room above, feet here and there, carpet to boards and back again. I know not why I fixed this hour. Seven-thirty is a pleasant one, twixt evening and the night—one when the scent of grass in summertime, as now, is as keen and splendid to the senses as in the morn.

Will you come uneasily, trailing your skirts, boots buttoned tight, the drawstrings of your drawers in offered bows that wait the seeking touch of fingers? I have never yet seen your drawers, nor thus the bulbous cheeks that

1

lie beneath, sheathed in batiste or silk, or a more common linen.

Your portrait hangs before me on the wall—the silver-point that Charles drew in the Spring. Upon my firm insistence—though I was not present—you loosed your bodice loop by loop, unwinding cord from small steel hooks until the pale-orbed promise of you showed. Agnes being shocked, or purporting to be, I persuaded her that many gowns are almost as low-cut and that Charles had long had a yearning to draw in the manner of the old French Court—of painters now all gone to dust. The selfsame dust as that upon the windowsill? I must not fantasise nor peck at passing dreams. Charles was much put to persuade you, as I gather, to utter up your gourds half to the light. His guile, not mine, was brought to manage that.

Shall I, upon your coming, read Miss Atherton's report to you? She of the soft relentless voice, the birch, the cane? Under her tutelage you appear to have improved much in your carriage. That Agnes thought you to be taking the waters with young friends in Tunbridge Wells is neither here nor there. She does not comprehend such things. After the two months of your tutelage at Miss Atherton's (the name dry as a fig that has lain too long in a bowl), your own understanding will be much the greater. I learned of her by chance, investigated her establishment small as it is, questioned and queried and related all to all before taking you there.

You will know by inference the contents of her cool report as well as I, yet would not read it with the same insistence of your green eyes to the syllables, the commas, words, the exact phrasings, the hesitations of spaces minute and yet discernible, the triumphs, expressions of doubt—though these last are happily few.

"Six strokes of the cane will now suffice in my view to bring her to fruition."

Thus she writes. I shall omit reading that sentence out

to you. However delicate the phrasing, bowered as it is by whorls of purple ink, fine loops of nib, trinkets of dashes, there is a directness to it that stems best from action rather than from speech.

What a strange creature is Miss Atherton! I may as well ponder upon her as you, in my waiting. And in yours. Most certainly she has a noble carriage, her years not yet two-score, hair brown as yours, eyes dark and seeking, hard as pebbles in one moment, soft as roses in another. The rooms were clean—above the classrooms, as she called them. Mirrors were angled to a purpose, bolsters, pillows, thick so that a miscreant might over them be laid were she to be caught mouth-burrowing between another's thighs, up-ended for the judgement of the sweeping birch.

Am I to judge you thus? I am minded first to palpitate you gently—to feel the springiness beneath your skirt's rear flounce, if you are minded to obedience. Before acquaintance with Miss Atherton's, you moved away each time I touched you there. So thinking, I have drawn the curtains back upon the view—the lowing herds a distant mirage seen beyond the hedges and the trees. Thus might you in a moment stand and contemplate with me the vista, fondled the while by my slow-seeking hand. *On verra, on verra, on verra.* The fruit has to be tasted yet.

Through a peephole to Miss Atherton's retreat—that noble enclave of high learning proud with books resplendent in stiff bindings, globe of earth cupped loosely in a cusp of brass—I was privileged to watch the hissing arc of cane, the flights of softened twigs. Not, of course, upon your own bared derriere, for I had not then led you to her mansion, but that of another whose face was coyly hid from me.

Artfully—though, too, with art—I was presented thus with one who then, unlike yourself, was not a novice. Even so, in play or demonstration, act of wilfulness or whim, her wrists were bound as in an act of contrition, humbleness, and ankles stretched apart by unrelenting cords.

Such, I gathered from Miss Atherton, was the beginner's path. She will have it that young ladies should be frequently bound and tightly corsetted. I am not come to such manners yet. Perhaps we shall, perhaps we shan't. Better that there were no "we," for then there is no "I" nor "you" but simply a conjunction flesh to flesh and thought to thought. Even so I tremble within myself and touch the dust the sunlight will not move unless I close my eyes to it, see not the magic.

Five minutes. Your footsteps slur above, though more quietly now for perhaps you sense that I hear. Upon the mantelpiece in your bedroom your ormulo clock ticks out the seconds to your coming as does my hunter. Do you think now, I wonder, of Miss Atherton's far house—that mansion of bared cheeks, of wails and sobs, mischief in bedrooms and the girlish relaxations to another's tongue, or are you caught between desire and guilt as I?

I should have a maiden here—one curved as you and nubile to the touch. Such imaginations haunt me now. Her breasts bared, she would wait, statuesque, unmoving in the corner where the dark couch waits. Perhaps I should contrive such things, though Agnes would be fretful at such comings, might question such a girl, her visits here. A young Cleopatra you might yet become, attired as was she in strange head-dress and metalled cloth divine about your half-bared breasts, your derriere.

Would that I could draw as Charles. I would draw you now, your nipples rouged and eyes delineated with fine lines of kohl. I should not yet place such reflections on you though, nor cloak you in them. Your bottom may not yet come proud to me.

"Be swift in your undraping" (so she writes), "the quickness of the hand thus bares the cheeks, permits the warning hand to slap and smack. Each of my darlings are accustomed now to this, and Elizabeth not least. Her name has a sleekness that befits her well in manner and in silkwarm skin. She has been rosetted both with finger and with thumb, becoming fretful, squirming, and yet held. You witnessed all my efforts in this wise."

I remember yes—at the peephole, at the peephole— the entry of the thumb into the puckered hole of that sweet stranger after the birch, after the birch. What cries that died from her as softly as leaves fall! How her hips wriggled as she did receive! Had your Assistant Mistress not brought a pupil to me in the watching chamber, blind-folded and made obedient, brought to bend before my yearning tool (ah, the exquisite suction of her lips!), I might have spilled into my handkerchief. Her duty done, cheeks flushed, she was led out.

I treasured then the silence of that act, the sibilance of pretty lips to prick, the tongue laid flat to draw the sperm within, thick-coursing down her throat in bubbling streams. "A fine, skilled learner—virgin yet—was she," was said to me most casually by Miss Atherton. So many months ago that was. That learner will now have been pumped in quiet of stable or upon her bed, bottom and cunny greedy for the juice that ardent waited on her quiet return.

Discretion is ever the watchword. I promise you such. Bare your nipples to me that I may suck the perfect tips that peep above the lace in your portrait. Ever, mean-while, my eyes stray to Miss Atherton's report.

"After the birch, her eyes grow slumbrous now. Apply it sweetly and without undue pain. Tickle between the cheeks to make her lift. Her mouth is sweet. One may flirt lightly with her tongue, though she starts away at fingers to her nest. In time this will diminish. She is well-furred, perhaps better than you think, a pretty pouting of lips between the curls. Ease them but gently till her eye-lids flutter, but follow first where my thumb has oft in-truded. She will receive you better there. Have none of querulousness or jerks. She must come to it and knows it well. Upon your putting of her to your cock, be rhythmic in the movements of your loins, not hasty, wild, as some. Be firm, for this is what she needs. Upon her last day here she played a merry dance upon my thumb, confessed desires against my urging lips, is ready for the fray, I do believe."

She does believe? Is it not certain yet? I have so little guidance in the matter, yet have much. I am as one who in a wood seeks out a tree whereon is marked a cross. Shall there be flutterings of wings, cryings of Agneses and twittering of lesser birds? Once when we watched the soaring of the crows to their high nests, I palmed your bottom for a moment. You moved forward from my hand, pretending interest in the sight, and then made play that you were called and ran downstairs and I forlorn.

"The rose that first is sprinkled will seek again the dew." So writes your mentor of the past two months. I have known praise of her from others, distant as bells that sound across the Downs and stir the senses with some otherness.

All is conjoined here—all shall be conjoined—house to the gardens, hedges to the fields, and buttercups afloat in uncut grass. Here, mouth to mouth and eyes to eyes, hard nipples to my chest and bush full springy up between your thighs. Ah, silk of your belly—I would swoon to that.

Two minutes. Will you come, or run downstairs, hide in cupboards, linen room, invade the kitchen, finger to your lips behind the cook, daring the venture of my feet in such domains? You are too old to play thus now. The game is changed. You are to womanhood, fruition and desire, bumping of nether cheeks to belly, lure of tongue.

On verra. My thoughts run away from me. The poker of desire stirs hot the mind and sears the edges of the caution I would hold, retain, keep in reserve for you. Thus one draws in the reins of Time and hopes in vain to hold it. I shall perhaps merely kiss you at the corner of your mouth. We shall speak of ordinary things, converse in part as strangers do who are not come upon decisions, have no morrows to embrace together nor count the actions of each other as a threat or promise. We shall look at old photographs, remark on this or that, my hand upon your shoulder.

I recall such moments in the past when my mother would sit on the floor in Eastern fashion, I standing as often as not behind her and peering over her shoulders with my brothers and sisters, nudging for position. Mother was the guardian of the velvet-bonded album and called such moments "an occasion" when we were allowed to see within, vying to paste names to likenesses and months to years.

Mama would correct us ever, as for instance if my sister, Hannah, called a wrong year to a likeness, and so one mentally saw the sepia photographs move backwards or forwards in Time and with a precision that placed them deftly in their slots. Such labels of Time, I deemed, were more important than the names of my aunts, uncles, great aunts, or the old servants who stared woodenly at the lens as though not certain whether to curtsey or retreat.

I hear your key turn in the lock above. Why did you lock your door above? It matters not. Staring perhaps at your image in your dressing-table mirror, you retreated within yourself. Come not with trepidation. I would not have it so. Is your bottom bared or sheathed? This I would know.

Your footsteps sound along the landing now. Glistening of moisture on your palm to polished rail of bannister. Movement of heels—a hesitation of thighs. How curious that you know your body so well and I have known it not at all these eighteen years.

Of course, nothing may happen. I am quite capable of laughing at myself afterwards about this. Perhaps it is not real—the report a forgery and laughter dying faint full leagues away. Even the arrival of a letter bearing a strange handwriting and whereon is a postmark that I cannot read, will at times make my hands tremble. I cannot bring myself to open it before I have lit a cigar or poured a drink and prepared myself thus for the trauma of splitting the envelope.

Such relief as is inexpressible sweeps through me when I find it but a letter from a tradesman seeking my bene- faction, supplicating trade, promising Nirvana. Fre- quently I cannot resist such calls, for it seems to me by the plaintiveness of the words that lie beneath—those which, not written but felt, have curled into the fibres of the paper and are still and quiet, invisible—that such men are at the end of their tether and may be saved only by my purchases.

Such apprehensions seize me now. I am not I, nor shall you be quite yourself. We are all too many, envelopes enfolded deep in one another, and no one but ourselves to open them. Hannah ever told me that I complicated matters all too much and learned not how to take a bird upon the wing. She would display her thighs to me and laugh, offering the columns of her ivory bliss to kiss, but never higher than the puckered legs of her drawers.

"You shall not fête me—another has, another shall"— so she chided me, though knew my cock full still.

Once in a flurry, seeing the creasing of the crotch of her drawers into her fulsome nest, I quick displayed my prick and offered her to suck it, though such was said in wildness for I had never previously heard of such a thing. I being but sixteen then and Hannah twenty, she laughed and uttered, "Pough! It is too small. I know a bigger one, Tom dear"—with that was giggling, up and gone, away, the promise of her buttocks unfulfilled.

Shall yours be? Once—before you went to Miss Ath- erton's and we stood in here—I said to you in such a voice as I could manage without sounding obsequious or enquiring that there was a pleasant aloneness in the study.

"It is good not to be interrupted," I said, although you knew we would not be. There are understandings about such matters in a well-mannered entourage. Agnes knows my ways. Outwardly I appear, rather to my surprise, to convey a sense of command. All doubts are within me— they do not cloud my face. Perhaps all of us are so. I remember that you merely nodded and that your lips worked for a moment but uttered nothing, leaving me to wonder at the syllables suppressed.

Had you spoken, I would have been as eagle to the lamb on every word. A mistake of course. Desire makes scoundrels of us all. I, villain to this piece, await your entry.

The handle turns. Should I draw the curtains, fold the room in gloom?

Entering, you hold your gaze down on the carpet and close the door. The voices of Agnes and her sister Maude beneath us in the drawing room are vaguely heard and gone.

Chasing apprehensions with desire, I take your hand and draw you to the desk.

CHAPTER
two

"Y ou have fared well?"

I ask what I ask for I know nothing more to ask than something mundane, quite beside the point and neither here nor there.

You nod and, having shyness in you, look about. All is as before in such short shrift of Time—stuffed birds, the rubber plant, the layings-out of endless words in books that nudge ribbed bindings to the cold, uncaring glass of a tall case, the couch that creaks and soon must be replaced. Dust in the corners where a thick brush cannot reach.

"Miss Atherton speaks well of you."

"Oh. I did not know."

You know not either whether to giggle or cry. Your eyes brush the movements of her pen upon the pages here beneath your eyes. Your lips part, close, and part again. Head to my shoulders so you stand, I conscious of the clouds of thought that speed across the landscape of your mind.

"A birch may not be necessary—so she has said, in her preamble."

The words tumble from me, spill and agitate like scat-

tered pills before I mean to speak them. Or mean to speak
them at all. I have no recollection of aggregating them,
preparing them for exit through my lips. Such is a hastiness I have frequently regretted and have never understood. Too often is the mind a whirligig that must be
stopped and must be stopped. But I have unleashed now
the leader of the pack, the key to all as one might say.

"Let me lock the door, my pet. We may better speak
thus."

You do not reply nor stir, hands folded to your front
and wait. Through your brown gown the lines of slender
limbs that upwards swell towards your treasure pot.
Mounding of breasts a wonder to my eyes. All that you
wear now I would peel away. Not yet, not yet, not yet,
not yet.

"So—we may talk, then."

Hands on your shoulders, I stand behind you.

"Yes."

Ah, how you tremble! Swiftly perhaps I'll have your
drawers down and removed, but wait upon your words
as one whose meal half served looks to the waiters, holding patience.

"Say that it was pleasant there, at least. Sometimes. I
would have you say it so."

"Yes, it was. Sometimes pleasant, yes."

"Sometimes, infrequently, but not always, yes?"

"If . . . if you would have it so. I mean . . ."

"Yes? What? To speak, if you will speak, yes, what?"

A blush rises on your neck. You hang your head. With
gentleness forlorn I smooth my hands down to your wrists,
then slide them up again to rest beside your neck. Crows
on your shoulders. Do you think of such?

"Miss Atherton stung me—oh frequently she did!"

"To a purpose, to a purpose. You needed the birch, the
cane, the strap, my love. Did you not, did you not, did
you not?"

Bemused, I turn you slowly, eyes to eyes, nose to my

chin. Are you defaulter from my dreams who speaks with
such naïveté, or is all meant to agitate, confuse—find
shelter in the panther's den? Your head sinks down, your
gaze absorbs the buttons of my coat. You would clutch,
if you dared, for safety. Do your cheeks tighten beneath
your drawers? Your lower lip sucked in. Head shakes a
little.

"I don't know."

"Do you not?" I quiet reply.

Were I to let you go now it would be an exit to obscu-
rity—mindless but sweet among your sisters, friends,
awaiting in a year or two or three the marriage bed.
Encumbered by dullness, you would lose yourself. Garbed
in domestic problems you would lose your charm—a
rose among the flowerbeds, rarely seen.

"No."

A small, slow stubborn "no"—I know this *no* for such.

"Then your learning at Miss Atherton's has been incomplete."

Blush rising and your head shakes more. Don't know,
don't know, don't know, don't know. I hear the humming
of the words within your mind. My hands glide to your
elbows, wrists again, slide underneath your hands against
your thighs. Ah, fullness of flesh and banding stocking
tops, transition from the silk to silky warmth beneath
your robe!

"Has your learning been incomplete?"

I have repeated in effect what I have said before and
may do so again. The moment is nigh upon us and the
door is locked. Agnes will not disturb and the servants
dare not. It is not known that you are with me, are within.
There is much sloth and carelessness around the house,
no thought connected to another thought, nor dreams to
dreams.

Phillipa broods perhaps upon her crochet work—the
elder and the still untried, too old now for the birch and
yet too unremarkable to conquer. I have not thought of

her before in either wise. Strange that I do so now, my
hands about your thighs. I am frequently thus, though,
colliding one thought into another, playing at skittles with
my intentions, posting thoughts within my mind but each
bearing more than one address.

My Aunt Sarah was such, though with even more eccentric ways, for she would write letters and cast them
on the floor, not deigning to address the envelopes which
she said was a servant's task. Upon quitting her escritoire
she would leave all lying about and after a day or two
would despatch a maid to see to them. The poor girl, not
being literate and unable to attach names to names, would
often address them to the wrong people which would
cause the uttermost confusion.

There would be arrivals of those not intended to arrive
and upon occasions when my aunt was not ready for
them. Once, a particularly intimate letter was posted to a
gentleman for whom it was not intended. He, being in
surprised hope of the outcome, duly presented himself.
By chance he had the same surname as he for whom the
letter was intended, and this of course had confused my
aunt's maid completely. Finding my aunt in her boudoir,
he set to give her that which he understood her to have
desired of him, she crying out all the time, "Oh, sir, this
is most impractical!"

The experience proved more enjoyable than she had
thought, however, and turned her—it was said—into a
wanton woman. Father told his cronies that he mounted
her himself several times after that, for she had not then
attained her twoscore years and was as bouncy in her
form as a new bolster. Upon my reaching the age of
seventeen, he gave me this intelligence in the form of a
jovial warning, though as much intended as a boast also,
I believe, for he saw much of himself in me and I suspected that his flute had been put to Hannah's lips if not
her cunny and her bottom also.

All is tentative in this moment now—hangs by a thread.

"Obedience calls for an answer to my question, Elizabeth."

"Yes, I know. Forgive me, but . . ."

"Your period of meditation in the twenty-four hours since your return from Miss Atherton's is over. Did she not tell you of such a period—apprise you of its purpose? Have I not been patient?"

"Yes."

A fit of impatience seizes me, though I regard it as a flaw in myself. My hands leave your thighs—abode of promise there—and I move back to contemplate the view, to demonstrate as it were my independence of this moment. The cowman and his boy are now at work and ponderous the cattle move.

"When were you last caned? Tell me true."

My words come quick, abrupt; a surprise to you, no doubt.

"I don't . . ."

"*When*?"

"Last Monday—Tuesday, was it? Oh, you fluster me!"

I have raised Miss Atherton's report and skim the lines, seeking the sentences I seek, assurances from her now far abode.

"After the brief period of meditation, and having given thought to all that has passed and the dutiful nature of her attitudes and postures in my presence, reminders are to be accorded to Elizabeth that her disciplinary periods are not entirely at an end. This she has been advised of and understands. Her willingness to please peeps forth already in her manner. I find her not mendacious, sly, untrustful."

"Your willingness to please, you see." I so repeat. That I am meant to read these lines out to you I am aware. They postulate, prepare you for acceptance. My tone in reading out aloud is stern, yet has an intertwining chord or two of kindness. You listen, stir uneasily. "You are well-judged, my love, you see. Let us then have fewer

hesitations in the matter. Raise your skirts, remove your
drawers, let me see your bottom at long last. I shall
accord you very lightly that which you must receive.
How were you placed for her towards the last? Over her
desk? Upon a bed, a couch?"

"A bed—a couch—no—yes—oh, I forget!"

"The couch, then. Is it not more comfortable that way?
You kneel to receive—on all fours, as I read, bottom
well-orbed and legs apart. Come—let me see that which
you have yielded now, though hitherto evaded my caress."

How sweetly the apprehension in your eyes beats wings
as might a bird within a cage. Permitting you a moment
of modesty, I turn to fumble out a cane so newly bought
and smuggled underneath my coat within. A rustling of
your robe brings blood to pound. Upon my turning back
again you have uncovered just above your knees and so
stand like a little girl who would display herself and yet
would not.

How curved your legs—how dimpled are your knees!

"Sh . . . sh . . . shall you cane me hard?" You eye the
cane as does a bird a cat.

"As to that, we shall judge your progress first. Come,
Elizabeth—higher! Show me your thighs, the lustrous-
ness of skin, the colour of your garters, crotch of drawers. Were you not so taught?" I swish the cane and make
you start a little.

"Yes."

"So taught by whom and to what purpose?"

"B . . . b . . . by Miss Atherton and she said . . . she
said . . . that upon my return I in all manner of things
was to be obedient to you, and that, and that. . . . Oh, I
cannot!"

So you turn, spin round away from me, your shoulders
hunched. I seize your hands that clasp the hem and with
a roughness quite undue draw up your skirts waist-high
to show silk drawers, the swelling bliss of thighs, pallor

of skin and surfaces of cream, beauty of bottom pert and tight.

"Stand so! Now loose the bows and push them down. Offer your bottom to me, girl, as you were taught. Shall you be caned more often than you need?"

"Oh-woh!"—the little quivering "Oh!" that pulls upon a drawstring and constricts your lips so prettily. Trembling your hands. I would not have them tremble. Here is no abode of fear, but love. They soon shall cease to quiver, I believe. When you are come to it, are come to it. Slip the bows slowly for I would savour every second of these moments ever on and would repeat them till eternity.

The waist is loosened. Your hands hesitate.

"To the couch, Elizabeth. Thrust them down and kneel. You know the posture well and have been coached. Down to your ankles, yes, and spread your knees apart. More slowly, though, as you were taught to move, and with deliberation, were you not? I entertain no hesitations now, you understand?"

I have breached a better sharpness in my tone, come better to the task in hand. Laggard you step towards the waiting couch, the altar of your offering. Awkward you kneel, your face aflame, and then at last your drawers push down, your robe wrapped like a parcel round your waist.

Ah! heaven's view! How chubby are your cheeks, the nether hemispheres inrolling to their cleft where thumbs have touched and tickled, entered in. So smooth your skin as is unruffled snow, and has a sheen upon it as of silk. Between the tightness of the cheeks a thin faint gingery hue as though to hint of fires within. Such slenderness your waist obtains as gives voluptuous flaring to your hips.

"Were you taught so? Should not your hands be forward, back well dipped?"

I must keep the trembling from my voice, adjudicate

on my intentions now. Least of all would I bring the cane to this sweet globe, and yet it must be so. *The cane is as a spur, an urging on*. Thus writes Miss Atherton in your report, and this I do believe. The hypocrite within me sits hands clenched, will not look up, will not, but waits the darling moment of desire.

In the moving forward of your hands, hips arched and bottom thrust, your quim shows now. Its peeping like a fig is meant to lure, the lips compressed yet rolled sufficiently to show the future promise of their parting. The nesting curls sprout prettily around, dark in their contrast to the pale above. Bulging you bulge, your head hung down, breasts pendant in chemise and nipples soft. A sparkle fleets across them now perhaps as, delicate, my hands remove your drawers and rustle the folds most swiftly off your heels.

I rise. My blood peals like soft bells within my veins. You are prepared and ready for the joust, yet even as a man in dreams I bend again and thrust your robe up high, revealing full the deep curve of your back that dips to make your bottom prominent.

There must be a moment of waiting. I am aware that there must. As a boy, listening to the chiming of the grandfather clock in the hall where the sunlight in the afternoons fell across it and rivered the wall coverings with light, I thought of the hours as ripe plums falling down upon each chime—falling and gathering beneath the pendulum. So taken was I with this thought that I would sometimes turn the key, open the long narrow door of the clock and peer within. It had always seemed to be that if I thought there should be plums then there should be, ripe and fit to eat as hours of sweet, enduring pleasure often are.

Your plum awaits, or better that I call it now a peach for such are often cleft as is your derriere, though never with such art nor depth. How should I cane you? Swish or cut or tease? Doubt of one's own intentions is often a

promising point at which to arrive, for some chance encounter, word, line read or new thought taken will direct
the path one's footsteps take.

"Your knees apart more now. Your drawers no longer
hinder you. Display is proper to your age and nature,
Elizabeth. Have no coyness. Let me see it all. Thrust it
now well up."

"YEEEE-OOOOH!"

No sooner have I spoken than the cane spurs in, swishing through air and now across your cheeks. How perfectly it skims and then rebounds as from a taut balloon!
Your hips jerk, thresh, draw in, thrust out again. A fine
pink line has seared the snow-white skin. Have I hurt
you? I desire not to. Your breath comes out like hissing
steam. Adorable your wriggles as you squirm.

*Let each stroke be followed by an interval that she may
absorb.* Yes—thus your teacher wrote.

I, too, am learning, as you see, will have no truck with
harshness, cruelty. Your cheeks quick tighten, then relax.

*Elizabeth must be told frequently to offer. She has a
tendency to retract her bottom. Her boldness is increasing very slightly. I judge this as the best of signs. Nurture
the tendency by stealth, design and flattery. Afford her
comforting progressively—until she may be put to you.*

I have read and listened to such words and shall continue to. Such "confessions" as you made against her
lips, I wonder at. A peach is no less sweeter for its being
taken openly or yet by stealth. Juice runs upon the lips
as ever would. As yours shall spatter yet upon my cock.

What whispered she to you in comfortings, her fingers
errant underneath your globe and flirting at your moistened nest? Perhaps you heard not her babbling well nor
true, mind clouded, bottom stung, cheeks clenched against
her slow, persuasive thumb, and then with gritting whimper opening.

"THEEE-OOOOH!"

I have given you the interval and bring down the cane.

Your cry comes now as might the calling of a curlew distant, heard, unheard. Young ladies do not scream aloud, as you have well been taught. A spluttering upon your lips, as of saliva bubbling through. Well quenched, well quenched—I would taste honey there or something more mundane as lemonade or strawberry jam, a wisp of crumbs upon your tongue. Such homeliness might be in lust as brings me to desire it more. How strange that thought! One dreams of boudoirs, elegance, silk curtains fluttering, and golden charms, yet comes to postures angry in their lust upon a creaking couch or dusty floor, a leg of chair that bumps against the nose.

Another waiting. These are not reprisals, for you have not sinned and know it to be so and yet are come to it. If there were sin it would be in refusal—or so I tell myself. Better such ardent days than those grown dry and unremembered, placed against a wall like old, used planks that have no other place to stand yet must be kept outside the house as if they did not belong to it and so are spurned in separation.

"Four more, Elizabeth, four more."

I have excused myself and should never do so. Your palms are flat-laid on the couch's wrinkled surface where the black of velvet has grown dusty grey. Your bottom rolls a little as it should in waiting—ardent as I like to think for the cane's caressing of your peach.

SWEEE-ISSSSH! A small, thin screech as cane meets bulge and sweeps up artfully beneath the deepest curve. "TEEEEE-EEECH!" your whine sobs out and dies away as does the whistling of the boys along the lane at morning on their way to school. "WOH-WOH!" your little cry of sweet despair.

The sounds are too imploring to my ears. I, coward, retreat, and let the cane fall down to clatter briefly on the carpet. Stung, you churn, and yet with bravery maintain your pose. Were I to reprimand myself, it would be for this last—too bitterly, too eagerly put in. The pink is

angrier upon your orb and all the clenching in the world
will quell it not, nor the insurgent heat.

"It is finished, it is finished, it is finished. What a
bottom you have, oh my sweet one! Rise and turn, rise
and turn. Did I sting you so?"

"Oh-woh-woh, yes!"

Blubbering you blubber in your turning as you turn,
tears brimming, holding close, cheek to my chest and all
about is quiet save for a sound of groom and horse beneath the window passing by.

"Hold your robe up still. Let me feel. Your legs apart,
my sweet, to let me feel. I may feel, may I feel, I may?"

A snuffling of breath. Your nostrils flare against my
chest. O moment of delight as I reach down and with
splayed fingers cup your apple, peach, proud prominence
in all its evening heat, future imbiber of my urgent juice.
O glory at the sting-sheened skin, velvet on top and firm
beneath, inrolling of the hemispheres. I part them gently
as you jerk.

"Be still, my pet, be still. Is this not nice? Nicer than
was nice a moment here before?"

"Uh!"

Such a sound escapes you as I can not distinguish—
yes or no—yet take it for assent than otherwise. So may
you well have gasped within her arms, repelled, at-
tracted, elusive in desire, haunted by images as runs the
mind when toiling, coiling in the dreams of sleep. Your
hands claw at my coat as swallows cling to walls between
their flights, small claws unknowing of the warmth within.

"Just to touch you there within—just for a moment in
your betterment."

Shaded are my soft, husked words as charcoal shades
the white of paper. Somewhere below, beyond, a gardener rattles spade to fork or scythe to shears as your
rosette I feel. Deep in the chasm there the puckered rim,
your breath outflowing and your fingers hook more des-
perately upon my cloth. So must it be, I know, and I have
no remorse for it.

CHAPTER
three

Once in my youth, my parents having guests—a few selected, combed out from the rest whose carriages had earlier driven off—I crept down to the landing, watched and heard, and saw a downstairs maid brought in who it was said was willing.

As it seemed—and as I heard it after put about—persuasions had gone easy to her ears and several sovereigns put into her purse beforehand. But then upon the hour she wilted, mewed, protesting at such sins as she was brought to. Of course, nothing availed her then, lamps being dimmed and she within the drawing room as hunted as a fox before the hounds.

"The first to split her cheeks shall have her twice!"—So went the cry and trousers quick unflapped while she to pillage by the ladies went, her skirt thrown up and made to bend before a table that was fit for such a sport, neck gripped and arms held out before her.

Her moans resounded even as yours shall, and yet she quietened in the end until her bottom frothed with sperm. Mama being caressed meanwhile by a gentleman, I saw her thighs for the first time, garters, drawers, and felt my cocky tingle, for all was sportive in such times and many

21

were the drawers removed that night to fete the corking of the maid. Mama was then hidden from me, though, and so I crept back to my room in wonderment at bubbies, genitals, and pubic mounds, droopings of drawers and cocks a-flash.

I have my hand now to the back of your head and hold you close in as a bird might nestle in the palm. My thumb intrudes between your bottom cheeks—the tight ring yields—a moan, a whimper from you and an inch is gained.

"Hold still, hold still—now, sweet, your tongue. Tongue to my tongue and lips to mine in solace for your discipline."

So drips hypocrisy as wax drips to a candle's heat. Yet I must have it so, can feel the heat emergent from your bottom's glow.

"DOO-WAH!" you choke your melting lips to mine. I have you thumb-corked, held, your seepings of saliva to my own, a fleeting lisp of tongue then gone again.

"A little more within, my love. Move on my thumb, press down, receive."

Scrabbling of fingers at my coat. "TOOO-HOOOO!" You are not brought to words. Too fogged within your mind they know not their escape. And yet your hips move now, a fraction down and then another with your breathing fast. The tight ring clenched about my thumb draws in another inch of it. Teeth chatter, nostrils hiss, and so you stay. I stroke your hair and fondle your rear cheeks with my free hand, my other thumb extended and deliciously contained.

"There good, there good—how well you do. Remain so, skirt kept up and legs apart. A kiss, my pet, once more, protrude your tongue."

Gulping and swallowing, your cheeks suffused, you tremulous obey and utter tiny squeaks as my thumb moves with caution in and out, scarce gaining territory of clenching warmth and yet not losing it.

"Work your bottom so a little, back and forth." Thus murmur I upon your darling mouth, and all is hazed about us as a cloud. I at a circus am—trainer to angels, cupids, dancing fawns. "The deeper that it goes, my love, the closer are you to obedience. You understand."

"Yeh-eh-ess! Soooo-OOOOH!"

Your mouth to my mouth open in surprise. Drawing upon your tongue I suck its sweets and fain would cup your quim to bring you on. Another inch. You jerk, but still contain—the silky bulge against my fingers pressed. My cock against your robe burns through such cloth as saves us all from hourly, daily sin.

"Do you like it so? Do you? Like it so?"

You will not answer—mutinous. I in my fortitude have shown you not my penis yet, the firm stalk waiting to invade your cheeks. Perhaps I shall bring you first to suck upon it with your lips in penance for your mutiny. I kiss your cheeks, your eyes, your upper lip, and then retract my thumb with stealth and care, bringing your bottom to jiggle as I do.

I shall step back slowly. The moment is meet for such an action, masterly. I step back slowly as one who, having lit a firework, is not certain of the taking flame, and leave you quite bereft. You do not move, head hung, your legs apart, a perfect bush crisp to your belly's gleam, the mound a little plump, rich for desire.

Your eyes have no look save their own, not dulled nor glad. Your tears are dry, your bottom scarcely scorched, the grip of you still tingling on my thumb. Garters of blue to match your stockings, drawers. How well for this occasion you did dress, fretful of unveiling yet as careful womankind all are, fit to be seen, inviting to the eyes.

"Lower your gown, my love, but leave your drawers. They shall rest here on the floor in token of your visit. Come, please my smile with yours, say all is well—emboldened to adventure and to discipline."

The shyest and most hesitant of smiles you give, though

eyes downcast. As a dancer might so you lower your skirt with unexpected grace, extending one leg forward to the floor that I might see the sleek line of your leg. I seat myself behind the desk—adopt positions of authority, extend my hand and beckon you to me. You will see my penis in its rising now as you gaze down, hand limp in mine, limp against the chair. Will Miss Atherton have spoken to you of the dark mystery of the phallus—that which swells the taut cloth of my trousers? Questions arise that I dare not ask. How came her tongue to yours—how deep within? Were your breasts fondled—did your nipples sting?

"Your bottom—does it sting still, does it true?"

"A little yes." You would simper if you could and yet maintain an air of wonder that befits the evening hour when shadows first among the trees dissolve. The wasps are still within their nests, the bees to hivedom gone, and far below faint clattering of pans as cook prepares the nighttime meal.

"It will be thought strange if I leave my drawers here."

"It will not be the last time. Shall it be the last? You will wear no drawers when you enter next, will to the couch and raise your skirts in perfect silence, offered and prepared. So it is said within that you must do."

I tap the report. You stare and look away.

"Is this not so? You must answer if it is not so."

"Miss Atherton said to be quiet."

"Of course."

I rise, our legs touch, knees touch, thighs. I shall fondle your breasts ere you leave. Shall I fondle them?

"Tomorrow at this hour. You understand? What is to do then? What have you to do?"

"Not . . . not wear my drawers, raise up my skirts and kneel and . . ."

"Offer up your bottom?"

"Yes."

"For discipline, for pillage and for comfort, yes. Go to

your room, prepare for dinner, hold your quiet. Be as the ivy to the wall, a wind that whispers not."

"My b . . . b . . . bottom hurts still." With that little cry you would cancel out my words like one who tries to withdraw a letter that is posted from the moment that it slips within the pillarbox and may not by anybody's grace be rendered back to he who has signed it but an hour before.

"It must, of course, until you learn, until you learn. What time will you attend?"

"What time you tell me."

Your face averted, eyes hold secrets still.

"At seven-thirty then again. Wear but a thin robe, chemise, your stockings tight. All this is understood between us now as well Miss Atherton intended. Go—for some will fret and wonder at your absence. You were to Tunbridge Wells, of course, and saw your friends, had many entertainments, did you not?"

"Oh yes, I promise yes, all this is said. Phillipa became bored with my telling of it and I did not tell her much. She knows the place so well and could recount it all for me."

You understand the purpose now but not the final act which soon enough will come to you, hips threshing, languourous in sin, spermed to the very depths of you. I feel your hips already thrust to mine, yet will not rage in struggle with you yet. Your second caning perhaps, or your third.

Nor do I touch you as you leave, must hold my disciplines as you do yours. I of the throbbing prick have let you go. Do you contain such innocence as thwarts intentions? Am I again the opener of strange envelopes that threaten lawsuits, interventions, acts of disturbance, invasions, a bellowing of mobs, arrivals of heavy men in heavy robes?

I lean against the door and you are gone, into those female parts of you I cannot reach, into a youth that feels

maturity a foreign country—thus a land unknown—and
sense not full the tinglings of the prick as mine beats now
against my trouser cloth.

I shall to Phillipa. What madness possesses me I do
not know. She of maturity at twenty-three whose limbs
are full, hips sultry, bottom heavy, brought not to desire
as yet unless some lout has saddled her in secret. That
such could be I have no doubt. Her comings and her
goings both are vague. I have seen her heavy of eyes in
her descent from carriages at night, have questioned
thoughtfully but not too deep and, scorned by Agnes for
unthinking ways, have gone to bed or joined the Romans
with Suetonius and a glass of wine, or Browning yet who
blusters on, makes fine of words and has a trick or two
at saying things that no man set to paper quite before
him.

I remove my jacket. It is better so. You who have made
my prick stand proud have left it so in innocence or guile.
The coat will cover it for the nonce in making passage to
Phillipa. I assume, of course, that she is in her room.
You would have known, but I dared not ask. Intuitions of
thought are stronger at certain moments than at others.
With women one will never know. Even those who play
with dolls are capable of flirting with their eyes before
they then stray back to dolls, new boots or bonnet. Ever
errant, butterflies, they come and go.

Tompkins I meet upon the stairs, towels folded neatly
over one bent arm. Her eyes are prim. Her bottom, even
so, is fair for pumping, but with servants I have not yet
the nerve for it nor ever shall. She would scarce be clean,
besides. One must remain fastidious.

"Your Mistress is in her room?"

"Yes, sir. Mistress prepares for dinner."

A sidestep and I pass her on the stairs, the moment
captured, crystallised and gone. I shall be well received
or not received. I do not know. I have never attempted

such a thing before, may yet bring scandal on the house, the roofs erupting, china smashed and horses neighing in their fear.

I should retreat. My hand upon the door feels moist as yours felt moist in your descent. I have never entered at this hour as now I enter now, not knocking, nor rendering preambles of sound that might advise a visitor. Phillipa will think me her maid at least. I have nothing to fear. My pego strains, balls full, thumb all a-tingle still with memories. Had I taken you now, so soon, so soon, the spell would have been broken, yes. Besides, I mean to nurture you, would have you tongue and lick my prick before it enters in your nether hole. How lewd, how lewd I am become. My senses swim. I am surely not myself who saw myself as wielder of the cane and titillator of your titties, upraiser of your skirt, remover of your drawers. I must make my way as best I can. One bottom seen invites the sacrilege I am prepared for on this instant, yes.

The mind, you see, will contain at any moment what it wishes to contain. I have at times become a perfect bore on this subject, yet being aware of it have blundered on. After her "conversion," my aunt Sarah was frequently heard to say that the mind was as a casket filled with jewels and pebbles, hairpins, furbelows, old dancing cards and knicker ribbons. She would have done better to explore that concept further, for there is much truth to it, save that the casket is bottomless though from moment to moment only the surface may be disturbed. On the other hand, of course, on the other hand . . . . No, there is too much endlessness about the thing. One discourses of such matters and one then takes tea, pours wine or makes escape into the garden. Each has his own casket and none will know the other's well—may find dead spiders at the bottom of it and old thoughts one would not wish to see revived.

Such cogitations are as curtain to my thoughts, contrived to veil what he is thinking even from the very one who thinks.

Phillipa turns from her mirror on my entrance. Her curves uncovered are quite remarkable and better than I thought, hips flared, waist tight and titties full and rich. Corsetted and stockinged as she is, I see her full. A sumptuousness of bottom, brazen cheeks that bulge to split the mid-brown drawers she wears.

"What?"

Her voice has a little catch to it. I smile as best as I can smile and lay my coat down carefully. She will not miss what I present to her, she will not. This I know. Empty the garden swing, her dolls' clothes torn or dirtied, put away, she stands in womanhood. Her nipples show.

"Lie down."

I draw her to the bed, which by good fortune is a double one.

"What?"

Sharper now her tone but her eyes are dull. She knows not whether to admonish, show amazement or fall down as she does, so richly-thighed that I will take my toll between her long legs yet.

"Be quiet. Let me kiss you, Phillipa. There is time before dinner."

"Kiss me? What?"

Some women, I have noticed, who are given to sensuousness, partaking of quick visions of the cock when all about them think them innocent, are much given to slowness in their minds when opportunity obtains. It is a form of camouflage, I believe, as are the curtains to my mind. It permits them wondering silence when their thighs are felt, their bodices undone, and even to the moment when the prick enters they frequently will not stir, but at the oozing jolt of it will struggle just a little and so by devious movements of their hips will draw it in. They are given to quiet sobbing sometimes—a sound very close to silence and no louder than the beating of a small bird's wings—averting their faces while the cock reams back and forth.

I have frequently thought Phillipa was such. Now is her testing time. My face descends on hers, lips touch. Ah, thrilling moment when the lips first meet and merge that ever before have only brushed the cheek! Her knees bent, legs hang down, the bed too high for her heels to reach the floor.

"Do you want to kiss?"

"Kiss?"

Even so in speaking she opens her mouth. I find her tongue. A little coiling back, but not too timid. Her mouth flusters, blusters, escapes, returns. A little gobble of her fulsome mouth. I pass my hand down to her thighs, she lying half beneath me now.

"Open them a little."

"What? We shall be found, the maid will come."

"Open them, for I tell you to."

"You never told me to before. OOOOH!"

My heavens, what a richness twixt her thighs! Full hump of curls beneath her drawers, the rolled lips felt beneath the cotton's veil.

"Oh! What are you doing, oh!"

"Rubbing you, my pet, where I have never rubbed before."

"You make me feel faint. You know you mustn't. Stop— oh do! Don't open my legs wider!"

"Wide as I wish, and shall you say me nay? Will you speak at table that I found you in your drawers and brought you down upon the bed to kiss, first kiss, I who have never felt your bottom's curves nor seen your garters nor your lustrous thighs before? You dream of this. Do you not dream of this?"

"I don't, I never did. AH! not my drawers! I never thought to do it with you, didn't."

"Be quiet—lie back—or you will call the servants with your noise."

"Oh!"

Such a little "Oh!"—a wobbly "oh!" as is uttered when the spirit of defiance is quick fled. Such a moment as this was destined, as some believe all moments are. I take small account of such philosophies but mount the moments as they come as surely now as I mount Phillipa.

Her drawers swished down, she lies supine, eyes glazed and lips apart. Her posture speaks of lassitude—the conquered one who to my prick will burn. I, having no truck with nonsense, lord of the realm, ringmaster, scout, trapper, hunter, remove her drawers complete and toss them far beyond the bed. What a quim she has, full bushed and neat triangular, the hairs a-flourishing upon her belly's curve.

"You can't!"

Her broken cry's not meant—not meant at all. I stand between her thighs, thrust trousers down and raise my shirt. Her penance—if there is one—is to see my prick at full stand for her. Gartered tight she lies in splendour, nipples all revealed, breasts bulbous over corset's top, thighs slack, most willingly apart.

"The m . . . m . . . maid will come." Her stammer tightly spoken lifts and falls as though a breeze disturbed her for a moment.

Most certainly, yes, a thrill of fear courses through me at the thought. That we should be found thus is unthinkable, yet she too does not stir, erupt, to evade the inexpressible moment when my penis shall enter her and there disgorge its pearls of joy to mingle with her own. The longing is too great, the veils torn down.

I do not answer her. Silence is best. Miss Atherton has the greater knowing of such things in certain moments of approaching pleasure. I hiss breath from my nostrils as you hissed to feel my thumb invade your tight rosette. Lowering myself in most self-conscious pose, aware of

every muscle, vein, torturousness of desires and apprehensions of spouting too quickly for the first time in her
dell, I bring my cock to thrum upon her belly.

"Let me lick your tongue—extend it—I would have it
so."

"If the maid . . ."

"Be quiet. Push out your tongue—further, my sweet,
the while I put it in."

"NOOO-HOOOO!" Her buttocks give a little jerk. Their
rich flesh lures my hands. I cup her full and bring her
lovemouth to my yearning crest. Her eyes are lanterns
crying to the night for dousing lest I see desire within
them that she cannot hide. Mouth of her lovemouth nips
my pego's head, thighs shimmering to mine and nipples
stark.

"If they . . . if they."

"Quiet! They will not know. Who is to know? Have
you not thought of it before, before?"

"A little . . . wondered . . . big . . . how big . . . at
night in darkness big, how big, oh-ooooh!"

"Tis but an inch and eight more yet to come. At night,
this night, we shall again, between your own sheets when
all sleep. A lusty fuck, my sweet, I ever thought you so
to be."

"Did you? You shouldn't—shouldn't do it with me—
how can you say, do—oooh!"

My own outbursting cry merging with hers announces
the full gliding of my tool within her silky-warm, moist
nest. Belly to belly, hairs that coil and rub together as do
leaves in storms, the plump cheeks of her bottom held
apart, mouthing of mouth to mouth in sudden splendour.

"Ah, my beauty, my big-bottomed one, tit-teaser, what
a quim you have! Coil your legs up strongly round my
own."

Thus sounds my groan. Her stockings rasp, take pur-
chase round my hips, her ankles crossed, tongue lapping
wildly to my own. Murmuring and heaving so we ride.

The smack of my testicles beneath her bottom's curve sounds in the bedroom whose once hallowed air shimmers intoxicated by lubriciousness.

"OOOH-WAH, OOOH-WAH, OOOOH!"

Gurgling her song, she grinds her form to mine as though this moment long had quietly brewed and bubbled in some far stills of our minds. The stinging in my cock supreme is spattered by her juices as we ride, rushing of her breath into my mouth and hands that claw about my back while distant in my thoughts I see you still, skirts raised and hesitant upon the couch. As though to fuck you both indeed I spur my charger on, flash back and forth and bring soft cries of pleasure from Phillipa.

"We are doing it, my love, am in you to my balls."

An oddity, of course, that one must ever emphasise the very act one is performing as though a conjurer were to explain his trickeries and show the rabbit up before the hat. Very often in repose, or having thoughts of lewdness in my mind, I have smiled at myself and others for this, for one so frequently encounters women soft of tongue and erstwhile modest in their ways who give expression to obscenities at moments such as this. I conjecture in my wooden, wondering way that such combats of Venus, coming often by surprise and being sudden in their ventures, surprise us with reality and—having a brevity that itself is sad and frequently self-defeating—must be scored heavily with accompanying words in the same manner that loutish readers underline a sentence here and there in books that ever after carry the rude inkstains of their passing. In snatching such forbidden fruit as rims the lips with tingling wonder, it is as if one stamps one's foot, saying in all effect, "I am doing it with you, really doing it, and look my prick is in your cunt and all is real, your drawers are off."

Such long pent-up desires must thus be orchestrated, as it were, though I have frequently in the past accompanied such shaftings by repeating endlessly, "I love you," while being less aware of the emotion than the expectations of my surging tool. This being the more delicate icing on the cake, women who expect such tender salutations only—and perhaps have seldom if ever heard the word "prick" or "cunt" used before (and all such are terms regrettably ugly in their soundings)—are brought to shock by spoken lewdness and quite put off anything thereafter save romantic gestures. The deed is spoiled for them, the music other than they thought.

Phillipa, I find, is not such. My amazement that we are upon the deed so suddenly is great. Her mouth a cave wherein my tongue explores is greedy for the meeting there. There is wine upon her tongue. Her loins pump fast as do my own. My finger at her nether hole explores, finds it well-ridged and open to my touch, blurred with a little moisture of excitement. Our mouths a-gobbling pass saliva back and forth, bed creaking and her legs gripped tight, exposing all her lovepot to my thrusts.

"Did you want to?"

"Yes," she husks.

"Always?"

"Yes."

A silence then. Her rivulets of bliss a-trickle down my deep-embedded prick, hairs burring, tickling, grinding 'neath my own.

"I always wanted to."

"I know. You are always looking at my bottom as I pass. Always. Oh, go fast! I want to, but you mustn't come."

How childish, how absurd such speakings are. We dredge the mind for thoughts that earlier had no attachment to each other but now are pinned with certitude upon those other beings who within us live but move more cautiously about the world than do our outer selves.

"I must come, must come, let me do it—in your cunt."

I shall never use that word to you, I trust. With Phillipa it has an animal tang, the roughness smoothed by her own flights of lust.

"Oh-ho, no, stop! Oh do, yes, do!"

Rivers of silver lit by lightning now. Fast rushing, gushing of our eager souls, she to receive and I to give. Pellets of wonder plummeting up my stem to spout within her eager maw.

Clutch-trembling, straining limbs, her legs grind wildly as I sperm her nest and bring her bottom squirming on my palms until down-sinking down we sink, hazed by exhaustion in my weaker spurts, her cunny mouthing petulant to suck in every drop. Then panting,panting, dying, limp. White wonder painted full across our eyes.

How beautiful her mouth in these last seconds. Sultry and soft—I lick it all about, last pearls emitted, squeezed within, tip of my finger in her rose held tight.

"I shall have you there soon."

"Mustn't."

"Was it nice?"

"Yes. Oh, you shouldn't, though. I never should have let you, oh the maid, don't let her see."

Shall I be jovial now or serious? Withdrawing tingling tool I rise, assist her up and palm her bottom while she shyly sags.

"No one will know?" Drowsy her voice with hope is tinged.

"No one will know. You will not lock your door to-night."

"They'll hear! The bed will creak—I'll be afraid."

"You WILL not lock your door, my pet. Be at your dressing now and calmness show."

"I shall blush; I shall think of it. I didn't think you would, ever." A moodiness of tone that hides her need for admiration, comforting, condolence.

"My hair is spoiled." A whining now.

"Your maid will see to it. There is time enough."

I pat her bottom sharply, turn her quick about towards her dressing table, stern playfulness inducing the right mood or such a one as now I wish to set. Her shoulders slump. I will have none of that. Concessions made in moments such as this are but retreats down a long, narrow path. She must learn, she must learn.

"Your door—do not lock it, Phillipa."

A mumble, but no clear reply. She will do in any event what she is told now. The act was too intriguing to deny. Firm, fleshy, full, her bottom waits the whip—had I the heart to give her such. The thought slow ambles through my mind as does a shadow or a wisp of smoke in large rooms when the guests have gone and cushions lie in disarray.

I close her door—have not lost thought of you who linger silent in your room and wait, or with such distance as you place between us now commend your mind to ordinariness.

Would such be possible? There are distractions here— shimmers of apprehension lest the moment's lost and I between the two of you will falter. Even however to think thus of the two of you is a form of treachery which stains the magic moments that I entertained scarce half an hour ago with you. Choosing to be oneself—whether this self or that, yesterday's ghost or tomorrow's becoming—is ever difficult. Your drawers, the cane! I had forgotten both and hasten now to hide them underneath the couch. Tompkins taps even as I conceal the baubles of guilt, desire, excitement . . . and illusion? What is here to fear?

"Dinner will be in half an hour, sir, with cook's compliments, for she has overdone the roast a bit, she says."

"Very well, Tompkins."

I am sure that was not the message. She has woven the words differently, perhaps in spite or tiredness or is hungry herself, waiting for leavings from the table after. Such things are done, I believe, but I do not enquire much into them. A strange congregation now we shall be, but no matter. Planks laid over a well conceal the deep, dark waters well enough. At the first sound of the gong I am down and take my seat. Comfortable in her comfortableness so Agnes sits. Being little given to amourous play these last few years, it will ever be the last matter she will think of. She has come to pasture too early, as it were, but I do not mind her so.

The wine is poured, the servants come and go. There is always domestic ordinariness to be spoken of—cook to be congratulated on the beef lest she thinks me angry at her timing. The dear woman cooks well, must be retained. I discourse a little on matters of the estate, though none save myself at table are minded to have interest in it. An undue quietness obtains that I must break—bring Agnes to chatter of her day's doings, the advancement of the chrysanthemums, words spoken to the gardeners, a mending of fences, a flourishing of shrubs.

You have no drawers on still? I trust you have not. Upon your brow is ease. Patina of the false? Your eyes are decorated with a modesty as neat as the two bows on your dress. Tinkling of forks to plates—the courgettes, raised, hang limp and succulent. With a furtiveness that I regard as almost witty to the moment I watch Phillipa bring one to her lips.

CHAPTER
four

In first mounting Phillipa who, despite her little outbursts and supposed confessions during the lubricious act must least have expected ever to do anything of the sort with me, I was conscious as often of that overwrought fusion of mind and body that produces both inanities and obscenities. It may be complained by some that an obscenity is an inanity, but I would not concur with this. Inanities may be spoken by anyone and frequently are. Many are excusable for they are uttered in a high flight of excitement (and on such grounds I must hence excuse Phillipa), but others are as often spoken by rote, as when for instance one is asked, "How are you?" by those who care not a jot for one's existence, present state, nor future prospects.

Obscenities are either crude and thoughtless, uttered by curs or screeching harridans, or are as music to the acts of love. There is a strange brutality in the nature of the words we use in fevered action. Frequently I have thought that it is so because we fear them, or fear what we are doing in some curious way, and so eject them, spit them out.

Most certainly I fear to use such words with you,

though not with Phillipa whose inner soul, as I now find, is hungrier for the arrogance of cock. I fear such phrases might adulterate your soul, or so I tell myself. I know not whether I am afraid to shock or else would keep you ever poised twixt innocence and sin. Better to say that both are true and close the lid upon such cogitations.

Agnes sleeps and will sleep on. In our royal manner we have separate rooms divided by a smaller one. It is styled a dressing room, perhaps once was, but I have never dressed there nor has she, hence with its paltriness of furniture, staid wardrobes empty, an abandoned chair, an upright mirror and a table with a shaky leg, it has become a barrier, a small space in the world having no identity or habitation, a loneliness of air grown stale over which I sometimes sentimental grieve.

I am not sure that Agnes would share my grief, save to please me. As some women do, she is settled in a nothingness of comfort and nothing pleases her so much as wine, three-decker novels and much idle chat. These mild activities enfold her, form a barrier against the world she feels remote from and so seeks inner comfort as a child might in snuggling down into its cot.

The boards creak a little as I venture out. I must chart a path, draw maps of all the cracks, the creaks, the groaning of old planks—will fuddle them with thicker carpets soon. Your door is here and Phillipa's further along, divided by a bathroom and a linen closet. Here prepare the angels for adornment.

Phillipa (awake as I well know) pretends to sleep, hip turned towards the door, lush curve beneath the sheet. She knows its curve—invites with this display and no doubt tightens up her eyes to hear me enter.

I have no need to hesitate, announce my presence with soft words, enchantments, presents or preliminaries. Doffing my nightshirt, drawing down the covers so to bring her thinly-veiled form more clearly to my eyes, I slip beside her, feel the nourishment of her plump bottom's bulge into my loins.

"Ah!" She gives a little gasp as though disturbed from soft, engaging dreams.

I know my Phillipa by now—she whose lubriciously snug cunt has drawn my sperm thick-flooding from my stem.

"Raise your nightdress, coil it round your hips."

"I should not let you, shouldn't—know I shouldn't."

"Raise it up. Bare your fine arse to me, my love."

Thus by using a word I have never used before and one that in all normal circumstances would shock her completely, I of deliberation involve her in the dark complicity of lust, for if she protests not to hear me say it then the hour is won.

"They will hear—I know they will. What words you say! Oh, the covers! You will have me cold!"

"Such nonsense on so warm a night as this! You wish to disobey? You do, you do?"

"Noooo! Do not touch me there! Oh heavens be, you're taking it right off! Ah . . . mustn't make me do it, no!"

Rolled on her back, she laggard lies, eyes hooded, breasts full ripe whose aureoles encircle broad her thick and pointed nipples with their circles dark and crinkled.

"Draw up your knees with legs spread wide. Obey me, Phillipa, hand to my cock. Come, clasp it in your fingers, feel the throb, rub gently up and down and feel my balls."

A whimper that disturbs me not breaks from her lips, born not of grief but of excited guilt. Forlorn in thickets of desire she well may be, but her furred slit is thicket to my own. The sheet is redolent of musk and woman-scent where her bottom has earlier rubbed. The furniture— dark wardrobes, velvet curtains, chests, a lurking mirror, her brocaded chairs—stands witness to the acts we shall perform, our voices sounding hollow to the wood.

She obeys. The first touch of her hand around my

straining tool is utter bliss. Her knees draw up; her honeypot awaits.

"How horrid you've become!" Her nightdress limp
upon the floor.

"You do not think so." Her quim, teased by my forefin-
ger, is already moist, lips puffy, stirred I have no doubt
by her own hand before I entered.

"Do."

The blurred mumble of her voice dissolves beneath my
kiss which of deliberation is quite tender. Her fingers
clench more tightly to my cock, though she would have
it in her mind that in doing so she holds it from her slit.

"Let me fuck you again, my love."

"You mustn't, no. Don't put it in——oh please!"

"I'll whip you, then."

"Wouldn't."

"I would."

"Oh, don't! You wouldn't really, would you? Never
have."

"Nor birched you yet, but we may come to that."

I kneel up and survey her while she lies the victim to
my whims and hers. Her grasp would slacken but I draw
it back, so pettishly she turns her face away and shows a
profile in the milky gloom that much has to commend
it——curve of cheek, peeping of eyelashes and the tilt of
nose.

"Turn slowly, on your knees, my love. Raise up your
bottom to me. Let me see it."

"Don't want to do it like that."

"You will. Or would you have me smack it hard?"

"Don't want to"——yet she does with awkward sloth,
elbows bent and shoulders down, gleaming of back, rich
gourds of tits, the bumptious thrusting of her rear. I slew
behind her with no greater grace and let the tempest of
my cock thrum out its message to her plump, split cheeks
where rubs my crest against her orifice.

"Oooh, no, it'll be too big!"

Inanities and clichés all, yet we are ever come to them. Such utterances, as one hears so often, are a pretended description, of course, and not a protest. The game is no lesser a one than that which Society plays out each day in mundane conversations. A faint hysteria and wriggle of her hips clasped by my hands, as if to assure herself the prick is mine. I shall not lodge it yet, much as I would. She must learn the posture even as you have, though not in such wise, but you will come to it.

There are two diverging moments, as I apprehend, in acts of lust and love. The first is when desire so overtakes the spirit that one puts it in without a further thought and reams away, hot-blooded to loose that which takes such short time to loose unless one monitors oneself. Indeed I have read of Indian savants, near to holy men but given still to intercourse with acolytes, who utter prayers and incantations during it and so delay the moment of orgasm on and on until the very spirit is released. One apprehends that there is a clear division of mind and body in such and that the lower may enjoy what the upper is denying, as it were, though the two act in concord and have some future meeting point, as old friends who have long tarried to meet and finally hasten their steps towards one another.

My delaying is of a different nature. I am not arrogant, I trust, but would have the female wait upon the act, have knowledge of her waiting and enjoy it. It is better, as the Chinese say, to travel hopefully than to arrive, though the arrival may be, as in this case, exquisite.

Phillipa has a superb derriere and, I do not doubt, knows it. Her hips are deeply curved into her waist and so permit her hemispheres to blossom out with all the ripeness of this summer night. She will pretend not to have had it in this wise before, but I am sure she has. Prising the springy cheeks apart, I see her brown rosette, ridged, crinkled. She would endeavour to deny its existence, attempts to urge forward from my clasping hands, but I draw her back.

Her silence is appropriate. Such hissings of her breath as come to me but underline her expectations.

"Don't!" she whines. It's but a token sound. Mutinous her bottom makes to move, is held again. I move my prick to rise up over her bottom until my balls nudge to her nest's thick fig. Her shoulders hunch.

"I don't want to do it—not in there! Don't put it there— you won't—oh, please!"

I answer not. She would not wish me to. Gripping the fronts of her lush thighs, I draw her tightly into me and let my receptacles press warmer to her quim. She will understand this, I am sure, as a mastering gesture and will take it so to be. A would-be frantic shaking of her head, then she is still. Words rage in my mind that I will not speak. The tickling of her cunthairs to my balls is in itself an act of hallowed intimacy as is the flowing and inviting warmth of her full peach's pressure to my loins.

"Wh . . . wh . . . at are you doing?"

Alas, she has broken the spell, does not yet comprehend the mystique of it all. I am above her in my flights of fancy, have not explained, would want no need to do so but am put to it. In doing so, however, I am bereft of words that would delineate each line of thought too torturous, too rich for her to follow, brocaded with such fancies as she has never entertained but may in time be brought to understand, as you shall know the spurring of the cane.

"Je vais te sodomiser, Phillipa. Ton derrière va recevoir mon pine."

What coyness leads me to speak to her in French, to tell her that I propose to bugger her! Thus I evade—for the moment—obscenities that are too crude to tongue. Sparse as is her French, I doubt that she has understood.

"Wha . . . aaaart? Oh, don't hold me so!"

Her interjection breaks the spell. She must learn by crudities or not at all. More feverish than I intend to be— though the moment now is nigh upon us—I draw my crest back slowly down her furrow and insert it deep until the plum assaults her darling hole.

"Ooooh, no!" A scrabbling of her hands to her squashed pillow, but I have her well, my lower arm full slung across her thighs, hand gripping at the outer one.

"Yes, my love, my prick in your bottom now. It so must be."

"NAAAR-HAH! OOOH-WAH!"

I cannot translate the sound of it. It is a petulance and not a shriek. Having offered up her derriere to me, and knowing well that she has, she knows better than to raise alarms, and so with majesty and thumping heart I urge within. Her ring yields, rubbery, and then receives. Embedded but two inches in, gripped in her spongy tube, I hold and savour the very lewdness of the act.

"Doh-oooon't." Another fretful whine.

"Shush, dear, and work your hips a little. Ever thus I have wished to put it to you, ever thus. Rich as your bottom is, it needs anointment."

"Don't, don't, don't want you to. Ooooh-oooh!"

Quiver and wriggle as she may, she takes it inch by inch, hush-rushing of her breath, then with a jolt I shaft her full within and bring her globe to nestle in its glory to my loins.

"Ho, ho, ho, I don't want you to!"

"You do, my love, you do—I know it well—have frequently unveiled you with my eyes, have watched you, yes, the swayings of your hips, long lines of legs, quim nestling twixt your thighs, and known you of an age when you would take my cock into your bottom deep, as now. Come, rear to me and work yourself until we come and then I'll fuck you slowly on your back."

"Doo-ooh-oooh! You make me naughty so—oh, not so fast!"

"Is it not nice, my darling pet, right up your bottom—say it now."

"Yeh-essss! Don't make me say it—ooh!"

Deeper I work and now she thrusts to me, hips wriggling forward and then surging back, squeezed in her hole and feeling all its throbs as so she does, the veins, the pulsings of desire for her. Or is it her? Would I as well be in your bottom now, or yet another's? I would face the question, yet cannot, and think of you coiled up between the sheets, an innocent to this as yet, or it may be that you have darkling dreams I have not yet invaded with my spear.

We are at full ride of it. Bent over her, her nipples burning thorns into my palms, full weightiness of her full tits adjudged, mouths meet, tongues twine, and sweet obscenities in our saliva spatter. Flowings of breath to breath and flesh to flesh. Smack of her bottom to my belly tight.

"Nice? You like it, nice, you like it—do?"

"Yeth . . . yes . . . oh, do it more—oooh-ah!"

"Right up your bottom? Spill my sperm?"

"Oooh, yes, right up my bottom, oh bad naughty thing."

All is said of course and nothing accounted for. In the night, in the night, the fevered night, the birds to slumber gone, the trees asleep, all stables locked, the locomotives still in their deep ironness stand, and hungry travellers in the bushes lie who know not bread to mouth nor wine to glass.

Her bottom's hot and clenching tight. So would I have had her as I have her now. Truly has she drawn a prick in there before. It matters not—perhaps gives spice to it, tumbled as she may have been in some dark park or in a carriage awkwardly displaced, arms, legs about, drawers on a dusty floor.

I rise, must sperm her in my full command, hands flat against her hips, my knees bent in between her own, her orb smack-jolting to my flesh. So dulled her eyes must be as mine. There is nothing here in this whirling time, this timeless Time, save my prick to her bottom while her tits jiggle, sway, and breath escapes in ever-rushing streams.

Let there otherwise be silence though she betrays it with her little "Ooooh's." So much surrender becomes her now. I cherish her for that and entertain the ever faster thrusting of my pestle while my balls snatch at her quim in little kisses of lubricious joy. Silence, silence, ever on, more meaningful than speech since it salutes the meaning of the act between we two.

After I have fucked her as well—after I have fucked her as well, my strength restored, balls blossoming . . . how greedy of me to think of this while yet my sperm floods now her ripe desire and she with a mingling moan and cry receives and sucks it lustfully within. We are dying, dying of our pains and joys, as ever man and woman do. I shall afterwards comfort her and nestle her in my arms, shall speak of her beauty and the warmth of her mouth, shall engage her in naughtinesses of speech such as I wish her to utter, bring her to giggle and confess her sins. Or perhaps I do not wish to know them—would create rather an enclosure where she may ever walk, drawers off, skirts hoisted for my coming, my approach.

But of course not. We shall return to normality. Upon the landings, in the dark where the lamplight does not reach, I will titillate her sometimes, feel up her clothes. I shall have her in postures absurd, palms flat to a wall and bottom bulbing out so that by bending my knees behind her I may nestle my cock up under her cunt and silent sheathe it in. Deep jigglings of her hips will assure that she receives me. A servant may pass, skirting us slowly where we huddle to the wall, averting her eyes. Agnes may arrive, her gaze uncertain in the dark, and ask, "Ttcch, ttcch, what are you at?" and pass into her room while yet my sperm erupts, leaps up, and spatters Phillipa's deep nest. She will thrust me playfully aside as soon as my pulsing's done, thrust down her skirts and exit to her room, not looking back nor making acknowledgement of our encounter.

We lie now side by side, my cock a thick courgette upon her thigh. Her mouth is sultry and at ease, quim rippling with the bubbles she has spent. Lazy our tongues—desire a long-flown bird. Sighs mingle and the days are all undone that knew convention and propriety, tea on the lawn, a peacock strutting past.

"Sleep now. Goodnight."

"Gooo-night." Her voice is slurred and sludged with sleep, though well she may be calling back her modesty in some pretence of it. Turning she turns, her hip humped up again and lays her cheek upon her hand, head burrowed in the pillow, dark to white.

I open quiet her door, nightshirt restored. All the world sleeps. An emptiness obtains. Monsters in woods—a flurrying of bats—my penis limp cooled by Phillipa's spurts when on her belly in our second ride.

Three paces and I come upon your door that, previously closed, now shows a chink. Your eyes for one fraught moment meet my own and then are gone, the door again closed tight.

CHAPTER
five

In the period of meditation that I always allow myself upon waking, not stirring save to lie heavy on my back, I follow with my ears all that is happening round about and within the house as though to assure myself that all is as it should be, that all necessary movements are being accomplished, as though the preparation of the household and its environs for the day were in the nature of some complicated dance to which the music is the bringing out of carriages for cleaning, the horses for watering at the pond, the distant shuffled movements of the cattle and, within, the would-be quiet and measured tread of servants, slurpings of water from jugs to bowls in bedrooms, the muttered acknowledgements of continuing existence.

It is at such a time that I make my own preparations for the day, the servants being in the main up by six and I awake at seven in great hope and expectation then of tea brought to me by one or the other maids, for Agnes ever changes them about—not greatly to their pleasure, I believe, but it is an occupation she enjoys and gives her a sense of manipulating the outer fringes of her world so that all within remains hedged, fenced and contained.

I remind myself, not without fretfulness for I had intended to remain within my own enclosure, that I have an appointment with Rutherford, a solicitor of no great talent though he is handy to my occasional needs. I have met him but twice before, having been introduced to his professional services through an acquaintance. Perhaps, I tell myself, I shall not arrive—despatch a messenger to say that I am ill. I have frequently done this before, sundering appointments and remaining within to pursue my window-gazing, ordering of the estate, entering of accounts.

This day breaks clear, though not so clear as I would wish. There rises, or soon shall do, in Phillipa's room, the fallen—or will she think herself so? I could as soon commend my prick to her bottom now as I did last night. Lusty and impassioned as she proved beneath me, I savoured equally my second threading of her quim which surely on wakening will offer her gentle reminders of our mutual pleasure. At the last she conceded that it was such, made offerings of her tongue to mine and at my lordly bidding did herself guide in the shaft that she would greedy sheathe, working her bottom all about until I was within and drawing on the sweet well of her mouth. At the upwelling of my sperm at last she wound her legs up tight about my waist and sobbed for it, and upon making her say that she had wanted me to do it to her, I. . . .

You!

I had forgotten your eyes. Could I forget your eyes, and yet I had. Blood thumps. I feel its drumming in my back, turn this way, that, within the tangled sheets, but have no escape from it, feel sick, forlorn, as might a man whose last sovereign is spent and knows no way to earn another.

Have you a knowing of what is passed, and shall I be accused? Not by others, but by you. Have you a comprehension in such things? Why I have attached or compared my fears to loss of money, I know not. I recall a fellow at White's Club, a subaltern who had got in only by dint of family connections, being taken up for stealing from the wallet of a friend who had thought to lend him money and had been about to say so. Thus I feel with you. Shall I say I was passing in the night? How ludicrous, for I could have come from no other room but Phillipa's. Have you such hearing that you heard? I have stolen from you, greedy at the feast have eaten off two plates at once and known my sneaking hand to be observed. I shall leave, take a town house, squander my money among harlots, whores and gay girls, will kill myself, pretend to blindness or some other affliction that may make you feel kindly towards me, yes.

Wait! Phillipa will deny, she must deny—but no, we cannot have such scenes. Certainly I must cancel your coming to the study this evening, though to do that would be a confession. Are you looking forward to it now? Does excitement race more quickly in your veins?

"Your tea, sir."

"Thank you, Alice—Mabel—"

"It is Connie, sir."

"I am sorry, yes."

The interruption serves to cool my mind, though leaves me little the less in trepidation. If in your knowing now you have contempt for me. . . . Dear God, I would undo the night (perhaps have Phillipa at morning in the summerhouse and no one then the wiser). Brave men crumble; I shall not. I have never thought of myself as brave, nor cunning, nor—quite definitely—devious. If I cane you not again you will think me weak. If I do you will hold me in contempt. All this depends of course upon your state of knowing, apprehension, imagination.

"I used your bathroom last night—an odd whim."

At such an hour? I would have made a louder noise. No, it will not do—it will not do at all. I have built sandcastles and have trod them down even before the tide came in. Have I not? I am as a spurned, defeated lover who returns again and again to his mistress, ever imploring explanations which she is not minded to give or would be bored to do so or will not do so because she has no desire to hurt him further.

What a nonsense! You are under half my age. I shall deal with you as I wish, restore the edifice, erect the temple anew, bring you to bend and have no truck with conscience. Yes, that is the best way. I am determined upon it.

"Connie—tell Mistress that I shall not be at breakfast but must make an early visit."

"Yes, sir. Shall I bring breakfast to your room?"

"Yes. Toast and marmalade will do—no more."

A capital idea! One that makes me feel quite adventurous. I shall be out and about before all are up, and breakfast not laid at any event until nine. I shall ride out as might my forebears have done, survey the fields, saunter by the river, cure myself by the waters, as it were, return for lunch and find all well. I may cane you even before this evening. Yes, that were the better way. You will learn by rote of stings, obedience, not to peep. I shall not attempt you however—but neither will solve the matter. I would have had you made aware of the purpose of your bottom's baring in a different way. By stealth and praise and coddling, as Miss Atherton enunciated. In rising, I imagine a conversation with her. "Be firm, be strong," I hear her say. It is all very well for her to say such things, but she has only the preparation of the matter, the entr'acte, the hors d'oeuvre of the thumb, and besides, titillation between females is different—is it not?

Perhaps she has trained you sufficiently already and I am only placed here happily to put the poker in. But I do not know, I do not know, I do not know. Rather you are likely to be as whittled wood that has not taken full shape yet.

At least the toast is warm, uncovered from beneath a serviette. I find myself, munching as I am (but having little heart for it) gazing with great intent and very little thought upon the wallcovering, the paintings, chairs, table, chest that all about me are. It comes upon me that I have done the same when going once to have a tooth extracted.

Of course this is ridiculous. I am taking no account of what may be passing through your mind, but only through my own. Hence it must be that I am plotting a false course in whatever turn I take, whichever route I follow. I shall have you yet. I swear on it, bluster and blubber as you may—but no, I do not wish it to be that way. A little blubbering yes, quite softly and with a trace of invitation in the tone, much as you were last evening when I put my thumb to your rosette and caused you prettily to wriggle. Your eyes grew a little hot then, I swear it. There was obedience. Surely it will remain? What an idiot I am—of course it will. I shall be neither jovial nor stern, but simply quiet and bring you quickly to the heart of the matter even as I have now brought Phillipa. It is merely the preparations that are different, yes. The mood will be the same—that is the trick of it. Had I but thought of all this earlier, I would not have needed Miss Atherton. However, and on immediate reflection, she was needful in preparing the first removals of your drawers no doubt. I would have fumbled that, had you not been tutored, made my excuses and apologised.

The day comes clear? I believe it shall. Cool air on my face and a horse to ride. Damn the crumbs. I have them on my waistcoat now and sticky. "Crumbs in the bed" was a favourite phrase of my Aunt Sarah's. Having been bottom-tupped, as I have said, and thereafter becoming looser in her ways, she would sometimes reply to some who asked her whether she had passed a pleasant night, "Crumbs in the bed," and say no more. It got about and was understood that by this she meant that she had entertained a gentleman and that they had breakfasted together in bed. Her moods alternated greatly, however, and if a puckish questioner should ask her on the wrong occasion,

"Crumbs in the bed this morning?" she would purse her lips and say coldly, "Certainly not," this causing great embarrassment to the one who had expected her to laugh and nod.

In reminding myself of this, I remind myself also that we should not assume anything, though if we do not and so fail to direct our thoughts thereto we can scarce be masters of our fate.

It may be, of course, that I could philosophise with you. Would you stare at me blankly or, worse, pretend to understanding when you have none, or would rather have none? I have known such things happen often—that is to say, in the ordinary way of life. There would be a silence, I fear, when I had finished and you would wait—no doubt with obedience—for me to do what I wish to do, but that would not be the same. You have not the hot-hipped animal response I found in Phillipa, the urgencies of mouth, the frottings of cunny to prick.

The house yawns with quiet save for the movements of the servants. Your hair is being brushed now, or you are sipping tea more slowly and more reflectively than I. A young girl's mind is as searching as a woman's. Do I fear this?

I have come full circle in my fears and have ever found therein solutions. By evening other thoughts will form, intentions crystallise. I'll have no nonsense: that must be the way of it.

I open my door cautiously, though have no reason to do so, and descend. To my profound dismay, delight, wondering and shades of apprehension, you are up. Upon the moment of my entering the morning room you pass without and stand upon the flagstones, your back to me.

"You are up early." So I speak.

"Yes."

It is a perfectly plain *yes*, quite normal, I feel. I must not make too much of it.

"What a jolly morning again. Do you not think so?"

"Yes. It is warm already. I am going to walk in the garden now."

A small quiet voice and gone. You are gone. Drifting across the sparkling lawn, a small startlement of birds, statement of sound, and then the air is still again.

I watch you go, back straight and bottom pert, one hand a-toying with your bodice strings.

All is well, of course. I can feel it so. What an adorable swaying of your hips, maidenly modest and yet made plain. Overt, not overstated. Quite adorable.

Even so, you did not turn towards me, did not turn. Surely I have always known you to turn and give a downward smile?

Yes. Always you have turned and smiled before.

CHAPTER
six

One cannot muse when the mind is over-occupied. Such thoughts as one would choose, extend, tease out, smooth to the finest of points, are as strangers in a crowded room, not heard above the brouhaha of voices in one's head. "My mind is overwrought—my heart is too full—I am filled with longings," so are heard frequently said. Curious that a surplus is always indicated when one would expect to find a deficit.

I am early upon my appointment, choosing not to loiter for an hour or more as I had wished. The waters of the Givvy, as we call the local stream, came cold to me. I fished for small fishes with my hand—found none. It was an idle searching—quite useless—indicating abstraction, stupidities of purpose, as though to draw the attention of Nature to my deficiencies.

Why did you not smile? At the least you might have turned to meet my eyes. No matter. I have already warned myself that I must not place my thoughts in your head and vice versa. By evening you will have decided to accommodate yourself to me, Elizabeth. I feel sure of it and increasingly so. The strength of my horse beneath me reassures me of it. He, lucky beast, knows naught of doubt nor of yesterdays nor morrows but only the chewing of the grass and a placid gazing at the world that is forever stranger to him save for movements, alarms, the comfort of the stable.

A dry man in a dry season is Rutherford, or so I take him to be. I have met him before only at a nearby hotel in the market town. I know his house, for it was said once to have been a Vicarage, but I doubt this for clerics do but rarely quit their habitations nor does the Church relinquish property. The outer bleakness of the house lends some veracity to the idea that has grown around it. The stone wall that encircles it has an unfinished air, being neither short enough to sit or lean upon, nor tall enough for privacy. The gate hangs at an uneasy slope, an apple tree here, another there, the tufted grass humped up by moles, and the garden beyond, around the house and extending behind having no touches of any landscaping skills but flustered rather by scattered shrubs, trees, conifers, and all so ill-placed on the sloping ground that they appear as uncomfortable in their dispositions as a girl whose hair is first crimped by the curling irons, her neck bent forward in fear of getting burned.

Three steps of a meanish aspect and a porch too dull for sitting in. Paint flakes unsteadily from the door. Are there intimations of poverty here? Clearly I am in a ragged mood—must not judge others by my irritations, my whims more secretive than I dare convey in daylight even to myself. Nevertheless, Phillipa was well worth our dark jousts. The bumpings of her bumptious bottom are my solace now. I shall, upon my return, kiss her and feel up her skirts and make no bones about the matter.

A single knock attracts a maid with such speed that she might have well been lurking like a spider in a corner, ready to scurry soundlessly along the hall.

"The master, sir, is out, I fear."

"Show the gentleman in, Hilda. Be polite at all times and think to the betterment of your betters."

Thus an imperious female voice sounds, though it has underlying it a strain of pleasantry, amusement as though the utterer of the plotted words had time to read them, brought a wry critique to them.

"Sir Humphrey Maddison, Madam, as was to see the master."

I am eased within a drawing room long and narrow in form and so cluttered with furniture, so furbished with furbelows, whatnots, stands, small tables, chairs, sofas and other impediments that I perform a perfect obstacle race to be greeted by a lady of imposing presence, gowned in burgundy, hair well-coiffured, being some three inches shorter than myself and a soothing of pearls about her throat that lead the eye, whether such is intended or not, to the monumental orbs her bodice half conceals.

"You are early, Sir Humphrey. May I introduce myself as Mrs. Charleson. My brother is not due to return for an hour. His wife is at leisure in or on her bed—I am not sure."

There is laughter in her voice such as I suspected there to be when she addressed the maid, a laughter not yet born but willing to be so and hence it bubbles like a spring upon her tongue though not in a troublesome or irritating manner but rather prettily. In time one might grow tired of it even as one does from the pursuance of some hobbyhorse which dull, tired fellows use to pass the time such as the collecting of butterflies—the poor things pinned and dry upon a board, their summers all forgotten—or philately which is even dryer and a new-found thing.

"In or upon, one may be comfortable in both."

"Indeed, dependent upon what one is doing, of course. May I offer you a sherry, port or whisky? Not here, though. Really, this room is a menagerie of stillborn objects, or at least they look so. We might retire perhaps to my own drawing room above?"

"Such would be a pleasure, but if I put you out. . . . "

"You cannot, for I live here—oh, forgive my stupid jokes. They have brought retribution upon me many times."

I preserve the remark as I follow her. Her robe, I see, buttons fully down her back to where her well-orbed buttocks protrude. A convenience should one wish to explore her upper parts, at least. My thoughts being roguish thus, I enjoy the vista of her rolling hips as she precedes me a little up the stairs. Regretfully or not she catches the direction of my glance.

"You must forgive my robe. It is an old one, put on in haste."

"In which you look most charming, may I say. I trust I have not interrupted your intention to change?"

"I may still do so, may I not? What shade would suit me best, d'you think?"

The question is unusual as between strangers, or those scarce upon a foothold of acquaintance, but she is patently of light and floating mind, friendly to the gaze and, I have no doubt, accommodating. "Shall we have a servant to pour?" Her question drifts like smoke across the small space between us as we enter her retreat, so fashionedly feminine as to delight the eyes. The drapes are blue and, catching the sun across their upper rim where the brass rings hang at leisure on the stout wooden rail, reflect a little of their colour up into the white plaster of the ceiling where it meets the wall. Two kissing couches face one another, as though preparing for some private performance, one with combatants, the other with spectators two. More space is here. One may wend between brocaded chairs and pass a sideboard, escritoire, side table, as we do.

"If you will permit me to pour, Mrs—er . . ."

"Grace, you may call me Grace. I am sometimes full of it, or have fallen from it. One is never sure. A medium sherry for myself, I think."

"You have fallen from grace? Did that bring retribution upon you?"

I ask without turning, uncorking and pouring as I am. I wish not to see her expression in that moment for I believe she would not wish me to. Such matters are delicate as between those of knowing minds, for so I already perceive hers to be.

"Are we to speak of such things? We are all but strangers, Sir Humphrey."

This being said to me as I go to her, glasses brimming, where she sits, there sitting on a love couch and my eyes journeying not without frankness into the delicious valley between her fulsome tits, I nod and smile. I shall not sit for the nonce. It will be impolite, but the Devil take it. I wish to be above her, in the ascendent, seen to be and judged such on the moment, fit or fair to take her as I wish.

"It has ever seemed to me that one of the most intriguing byways of life that may be followed, explored a little though not to the uttermost depths or ends where in any case trees often draw together and defend the further view, is that wherein comparative strangers enter into a moment of mental intimacy as water is poured suddenly from a bowl and splashes all about."

Her eyes dance. A slight wobbling of her breasts that stirs her pearls.

"Indeed? Then you should lock the door perhaps. It would have been unseemly had I done it myself."

I carry my glass. It has brought me good fortune perhaps. The key turns in a lock well-oiled, prepared for such adventure, soundless and discreet.

"As to retribution?" My stance retaken before her, I proffer the question again.

"You are in fine fettle, sir. Perhaps you had a better night than I and live still in the cobweb of its dreams."

"You have not answered, Grace."

"Oh, as to that, I may. You will tease me first, will you not? I was ever teased, made play with, tousled, caressed, a feather tickled up between my thighs. Sternness did not enter into it until the last. That was a way of things that we had. I speak of my girlhood, of course, though latterly—beseiged, it seems, by a constant vision of my presence and seeing me occasionally, not by invitation but by peeping, I do assure you in my corset—Harold has taken it upon himself to further my education after many years."

"By attending first to your bottom?"

"The naughty man has a tawse. Have you never seen one? Broader than my palm and thick."

"He takes your drawers down?"

I for my part have drawn her up, breasts to my chest and sherry on her tongue.

"How else may one unveil the altar? Have you not been at Vespers yourself in the night? There is a roguishness in your eye that speaks of it."

Tongue—dear god, she has a tongue that sets my veins on fire! Lazing, flicking, urgent, sweet, all things together. We exchange salivas as I grope her bottom, feel its bulge, the deep elasticity of the firm cheeks. I seek her dress buttons at the back. Her elbows fret and push my hands away.

"Don't! Will you spoil it all by urgent gropings? Ever was I fully-dressed for it—that was our way. Not wearing drawers, there was convenience in being taken to one's bedroom quick. Have you no feather? Feather me with words. Who were you at last night that has put you in such a froth? Wait—let me feel your cock and draw it out. Raise my skirt slowly now and bare my bottom. Put your finger up."

"Ah, devil, sorceress and witch, what fulsome cheeks, what warmth, what plenitude!"

"Darling, what a prick! Come, what was it at? I have a great curiousity about such things. You have not told me yet. I adore to hear—could never be taken in full heat until I had learned what my sisters, aunts or others had received the night before."

"Phillipa? Yes."

In overwrought excitement—a state I constantly coax and coach myself not to enter—the name, dear name, escapes me, tumbles out, spilled down between the weighty tits I fondle with my other hand. A curse, a blessing, be upon the knowing hand that weighs my balls and then enclasps my prick.

"Phillipa? Who else?"

Her laugh is husky, taunts, dismays, for though she knows her not it is as if she knew her now, could single her out by the breadth of her bonnet, the hem of her skirt or the lilt of her hips, the lustre on her waiting lips.

"How old—how old is she? Are you a riding master both of fillies and mares?"

"Twenty-three."

We are to exactitudes. I know the way of it. It does not matter, though. I shall have Phillipa change her name or use her second one, hide in the summerhouse when callers call, disguise as a milkmaid or pretend to be a visitor, a basket on her arm, flowers in her hair and all about her such a look as speaks of tight virginity.

"And the other? Is there another? Two, three, four or five or six? Oooh! you are too quick!"

"Be quiet, woman. Bend over. Place your palms down flat, present your bottom!"

I have her turned and over, hands upon the silk warm covering of the love couch where she has just sat, skirt piled to hips and her derriere full bared. A majesty of full moon here, the cheeks both suave and plump and rearing out in readiness to receive their due. No drawers. An excellence of forethought.

"I was not ever to be quiet. Am I to be quiet? Harold has naught to say. Furtive and breathless he puts it in, my bottom hot-scorched from the tawse. There are necessities in naughtiness, are there not?"

"I believe so."

I nestle my plum to her nether hole, nudging but not

entering yet and hold her so. The pose is thus erotic, lewd. We are at readiness, thoughts flowing fast. She snuffles softly, legs apart, is well-taught, waits upon the moment.

"Tell me! I have told you."

What girlishness is here apparent, yet it pleases.

"What would you know?"

I can tease as well as she, cock pulsing as it is impatiently.

"How did you . . . OOOh! . . . do it to her?"

One inch inserted of my peg, hot corker worked between her cheeks. Tight she is, but they are all so, ever there, know how to squeeze, constrict the muscles and excite so that one is put to it as in endeavouring to replace a swollen cork within a bottle neck.

"Like this, my dear, warm-bottomed on her bed."

"Did you wh . . . whip her first? THOOO-OOOH! Oh yes, oh push it slowly up."

"The cane, my pet, though had to tie her first, gag her sweet lips. She was rebellious as young ladies often are."

I grit my teeth. Her suction deep appears to draw me in though in all reality it is the increasing pressure of my loins. She cedes—bulbs up her plump, full bottom more and has me half embedded in a trice.

"How I would love to have see . . . see . . . seen that. AH, you beast, you are filling me up!"

"And caned her? Would you have caned her, too?"

I remind myself to beware of recklessness, fire in my veins and words that whirl as leaves about the face in winter storms, cryings of mariners and her bottom heaves now as the water heaves. I shall not be drawn to it, shall not, shall not accomplices obtain, secrets betray nor curtains lift. Even so I know the perils I am at, surgings of lust, the inexpressible moment as now I bury my shaft deep in her and let it pulse within her ardent grip.

"Let me! Will you let, oh let me, let? Is she not pretty? Did you have her well, mewing and moaning as you took your toll of her? I will cane her sweetly, ardently, my love. OOOh! ram it in, go faster, faster, love."

One regrets the paucity of language in such moments, yet we are ever come to it, down to the rockbed of the inevitable, the gargled utterances of the obvious, the words made plain upon the tongue, spilled like small hard pebbles from between the teeth. Such incantations it seems are necessary, as I have said before, in proof of what one is doing or evidently so. Or else such words lie fallow in the best of us, waiting to be spilled while by others they are used as imprecations—I refer to the lower levels of society, of course—swearwords, food for hatred, and thus two opposites are brought together in the very language of *amour*.

Her bottom bounces to me now slap-smack and swinging of my balls beneath her quim. Toiling I toil and yet have your image ever before me. Your bottom will be tighter yet, a smaller apple to me or a peach worked back and forth by my strong mastering hands, the cheeks squeezed tight against my ramming shaft.

"Do me! Oh do me!"—so her moan. I am the silent one, come conqueror now and rearing at the hillocks of her bum. I shall come soon, squirting deep into her depths. Her bottom rolls, rotates, extols, squirms to my belly tight, jerks back and forth.—"I want to cay-cay-cane her"—so she chokes, some misty wonders in her mind a-spinning. Rather perhaps she would cane herself for her deserving sins.

"You shall, you shall."

Such visions come to me as I would reject, should spurn, and hunt with scorpions. I cede that which I should not cede in so speaking, yet my cock is spurred, has wings of long desire. No promise made in such moments may not be broken. Some women when in the throes of lust are as prone to give their souls away as are men, yet once having drawn the sperm and having pleasured themselves several times and lying back within the enclave of a returning world such as comes mistily to the eyes in aftermath, colliding of curtains, light and windows to the eyes, or trinkets fallen in the amourous combat, will retreat behind the doors of mind they ever in their daylight hours keep closed. Such as has been spoken, offered, molten on the tongue, is as smoke in the wind, a dying of the moments past that had no birth save within the mind.

"Then you shall take her bottom —I her cunt with my long-licking tongue."

"While over you she bends, mouth to your quim, her hot-streaked bottom full surrendered to me, yes."

Our course is almost done. Passing my hand down frontwards to her fur, I feel her tricklings, spillings, spurtings on—hear in her breathing the escaping feet of devils.

"Say we will do it, say it, yes! Ooooh! You are coming now, so warm and thick."

A cry escapes me as she clenches tight, my finger tipped within her oily slit and all a-pumping, pulsing, melting into snow. Last gritting sounds and all is almost done. Faint far within her bottom do my pellets spurt and then as wingless birds droop down, and sound her moans as music to my ears. A fervent, febrile movement of her limbs to mine and then with steady suction is the cork withdrawn. She stumbles forward, falls, lies on her back and holds her skirt up for my delectation. I slump and sit beside her near, bent leg, her smile as artful as a jackdaw's swoop.

"Such an accomplishment so soon! Are you ever so?"

The poacher to the poacher speaks, of course. I trail my finger up her knee, beyond her leg, toy with her ruffled garter, look absurd no doubt with cock a-droop, a sperm-tear at the tip her finger catches.

"Harold has you frequently? As to his wife?"

"We play our games. Do you not do so? She has a letch for watching now, as I have ever had, was coy at first but soon persuaded. Would soon as put his prick to me as to herself while I the fretful one do play, ever squirming, crying all about—but showing well my bottom and my quim, of course. You may play with us if you wish."

I shake my head and smile. The stepping stones are dangerous here, uncounted in the dark.

"Then I may play with you? With Phillipa?"

A curse again upon it that I ever mentioned her name. I have a sensation, though, that Phillipa might—brought to the deed of it in twisted sheets. Beware the heated mind that races on.

"It would not be possible."

My tone is grave. I rise to button up myself but her hand stays me, casts my fingers hence and gropes my thick, limp tool.

"It would not? Let me suck it."

"No—you—AH!"

It is too late, the spermy plum engorged, within is sucked and tasted, rolled about. The magic lanterns of her eyes peer up at me. Sparkles of fire that would fearsome burn me yet. Where are the yeomen, waiting guards, to rescue me?

"I could make you."

"No." I thicken, tingle, rise. My prick upstemming spears across her tongue, my balls couched on her subtle, coaxing palm.

"Or the other one? Is there not another one? There is another, younger, older, sweet, untried, and ready for the fray, I'm sure. May I not cane the tightest of the bottoms while you ready stand? How heavily you breathe! Do not come again too soon. You will not, will you?"

"Suck it then, if that is your wish."

"I sometimes wish, sometimes do not." Her mouth withdrawn, she shakes her head, lolls back and gazes with amusement at my ready prong. So soon has never stood my prick before, so soon. Is there witchcraft here? Do my ancestors speak in shades behind me, clutch at my elbows? My mother was always mindful of witches, goblins, ghosts, would not have screens upstairs lest, she said, one hid behind one. My father would pooh-pooh the idea and of a purpose leave the wardrobe doors open in the night like huge bats' wings which frightened her as much, whereat she would have to rise and close them, believing something would emerge from behind the furs, the hanging dresses and the coats. Then would come a tumble and a tumbling for he would seize her out of bed, having a great and strange letch for doing it on the floor, upping her nightgown and putting it in a trice so that with the open doors immediately behind her she would cling to him, a-begging with her bottom slaps against his balls to be released. I heard this once, should not have done but did, ear pressed against their door and all a-wonder. "Come—you will come the quicker now," was said to her and from such noises as ensued I guessed this to be the case for her cries were different and so seemingly one emotion took links with another. Thus is one guided by events without knowing the reason for them, which is to say the mechanism or the chemistry, as alchemy performed without a wand or chant, bells, bones, or papers written on.

Grace has me well—I at an impasse with my prick wet, teased and swollen. I bend, one knee upon the sofa's edge, and bring the bulb of it against her lips. Her tongue peeps out, swims round the tip, then is withdrawn. She laughs and turns her head as might a girl who flirts between the doing and the not-doing of it. Such a vision indeed enters my mind and enchants. I think of you, of course—I think of you, Elizabeth.

"Let us talk of it, and then I may." Her eyes, averted, count the patterns in the carpet's mass. Hand reaching up, she gently works my prick.

"Of what? What shall we speak of, speak?"

"Of the impossible, of course, my pet. Is that not the most desirable to achieve? As to Phillipa . . ."

"No!"

Even now I am capable of objecting, refusing. I must leave. My horse needs watering, there are duties to be done. I seek for them but find none for the moment. I wish not to be confronted by Rutherford, might see him with his trousers down, obscene, or at the least absurd, unwanted as a cold bath in the rain.

Yet I remain, and wish I did not, wondering as ever who the "I" is that commands the "I," why I am two, yet one, yet many.

"Is she pretty?"

"Who?"

"The other one. My darling, let me suck it once again. We shall soon come to the talking of it, I know we shall. All will be arranged. You do not know me yet."

"I. . . . AAAARGH!"—my stem full taken in her mouth, her eyes a cornucopia of desire.

"Come on, you naughty man, come on!"

"Her name . . . her name . . . her name is . . . FOOOOOO!"

CHAPTER
seven

Being aware of the comical nature of my vocal explosion in that moment, accompanied as it was by a gushing up from my receptacles and through the throbbing stem of my organ thus splashing upon the tongue of Grace and finding home in her thirst, I perhaps appeased or mollified my conscience in that I had all but uttered your name. Yet at the same time, and all occurring with the lightning nature of one's thoughts, I saw less solemnity in my intentions as regards yourself than hitherto. It may be of course that I am in part a romantic, am much given to mooning over innocence, movements of lashes seen as baby butterflies upon the very cheeks that frequently hem in lips of particular mischief.

The highest art of Woman is to blend the attributes of wife, mistress, mother, sister, daughter, friend, mother-confessor, whore and lady——all. Grace possessed all these, as I was to discover, but it was by no means such a slow course of discovery as one is bidden to take by tiresome novelists who would have one follow a him or her through countless barricades of chapters, by which time one has grown rather tired of them or is aware that one is about to discover that they have merely made a fundamental change or changes in their characters that one not only wished them to but would have had them do at the beginning.

I, getting about, sitting down again, affecting bravado, yawn and stretch my legs. Unspeaking, Grace pours port wine for us both, sits beside me and—with pleasure evident—swills wine around within her mouth then lays her head upon my shoulder in seeming seeking of protection but really to peer into the corners of my mind.

I shall light no lamps—I swear I shall not.

"She is too young?"

"How persistent you are! Are you ever so?"

"We may ride together if you wish. It will invigorate us both. Much was seen to such manners and means and ways of exercising in my youth. Riding warms the bottom, stirs the hips, revives the generative powers, thrills through the loins and sets the nerves a-tingle. When after such I was led to a stable with my horse. . . . She is very pretty?"

"Of course. Who? You are a very devil with your questions. In a stable were *you* put? Did you say *put*?"

"Young ladies should be ever put, my dear. They know not in their coyness, shyness, desirings of fulfilment, how otherwise to place their limbs themselves. Have you fondled her not at all?"

"Very well, then, put. How were you put?"

"In one or another mode, my pet, dependent on my state of readiness to entertain the lordly cock, precursor of my being—that which as custom has it would renew its powers two, three and fourfold in my dell."

"Did you not struggle? Were you strapped or birched or had your bottom stung by tip of schooling-whip, or what?"

"Who now is at the questions as a schoolboy at the jam? I shall not bore you with my beginnings. Suffice to say that I had learned a little of the art, had my first

pumpings on my bed, being in the drawing room first
teased, then taken up. Being at fifteen and I the last to
take the manly juice. . . ."

"Fifteen, by Jove! How early you were taken up!"

"I had a fair bottom for it then, my titties firm as
pumpkins full, with pretty, pointed nipples that were much
sucked for the pleasure of it. Is she then younger?"

"By some five years yes . . . look here! I say!"

"Good heavens, what a fuss you make of it! Papa had
had my bottom ten score times by then, much fêted me,
and doused my quim upon my sixteenth birthday. As to
the stable, there I took my learning, cock to bottom half
an inch or so urged in each day until I could receive it
all, was made to stir my hips, rotate, draw in the sperm
and so receive my sustenance. Plumper did my cheeks
grow, as my sisters' did, received caresses, kisses, tongues
within. Amid all was the birch, the tawse, the cane ad-
monitory. I did not mind it so. It made me all the hotter
for the fray. Kiss me, my pet, the memory of it stirs.
Have you not felt her darling cheeks as yet—this sweet,
mysterious one you will not name?"

"A little, yes."

Confound the woman! She not so much teases as
squeezes it out of me, yet makes such game of it as lures
me to join in. I am, after all, within my own protection—
may close my own front door on whom I wish and bid
all to the devil go.

"She did not jerk away, nor raise a cry? You may
proceed then with her—perhaps with my assistance if
you fear the consequence of taking down her drawers." I
cannot help be but amused. Her voice now soft and soothing warms my ear—has the lure of a fire on a winter's
day when one should be setting out on journeys.

"I have not thought that it would come to that, my
dear."

"You have not, Humphrey? More's the pity, then, for

clearly you are set to tease more than to flatter her. Another one will have her first, of course. It is always the case."

"You think so?" My naïveté spills out. I who would master be am over-softened by her wiles and yet there comes to me—upon her special pleading as it were—a vision of you from a carriage descending late at night in the shadow of dear Phillipa as might be said. Perhaps you would do such from revenge? The thought strikes chill for now I know not as to the colour of the cloak Revenge might wear—that of neglect or jealousy? And time moves forward ever to the evening now, your portrait my accuser on the wall.

"If you disdain my help. . . ." Grace rises and smooths down her robe. Her voice, flecked with scorn and tinged with sorrow, drips scorn upon my seeming weakness, putting on my heads alternately the hats of creditor and debtor.

"It is not that."

I rise in turn and, close behind her, cup her breasts. Her head turns, flecks a kiss upon my cheek.

"So might I hold her while you kiss her, raise her gown, fondle her thighs, feel all about. In thus wise have I frequently brought young ladies to the couch or bed."

"You have done?"

Why must I unceasingly ask, be drawn to habits of the lewd? I should stride away, make my excuses and begone, rattle the treads of stairs with my departing feet and ride authoritatively beyond, away. Yet it strikes me then that Grace might have the impudence to call, invade my den, bring matters to a head, though such would not be impudence so much as mischief.

She turns within my arms, enfolds my neck.

"What think you then as to her future pleasures? Should she enter wedlock all unprepared and with bemused, bewildered mind first have her nightgown raised? Does one not polish apples first, pluck stalks from strawberries, garnish lamb before it is brought to table? Let there be laughter in her bed, not tears. Such as those whom I have brought to it have ever known the pleasure, not the pain."

"An inch or two, you said at the time, in your beginnings?"

I stir my thumb and mark its memories.

"If you would have it so." A silvery laugh. "In truth, it went half in at first and then he spouted. I wriggled overmuch, I do believe, was birched for it and made to mend my ways, then feather-teased was brought to spill my pleasure. Bring her to me. I will mollify her much."

"You would cane her?"

"Perhaps. The stinging brings desire into the cheeks. Her tongue will utter sweetness to your own, if you but let me. Bring her close to suppertime. Dear Harold and his wife will both be out."

"You are certain?"

"Of course! You will have spermed her ere you both depart. Who is to be the victor here? Not you—but she!"

"I understand you not!"

"You will, in time. At seven, shall we say? Upon the hour?"

"In truth I am doubtful of the matter, and besides. . . ."

"Harold will be here soon. You do not wish to meet him now? Of course not. Go, my dear, and bring the winds of heaven when you come again as yet will warm us all about and make a trio of great jollity and ease."

I do not answer. What is there to say? The winds of heaven indeed! She has read overmuch of purplish prose or sees her role as heroine. To *my* needs? That I doubt, and yet she was generous in her yielding—much as might be said did place a mackerel at morning to catch a sprat at evening. Nevertheless I must be circumspect and clear my head. In snatching you from the roses where for all I know you wander still I may well tear my hands that seek your warmth. Then would you have the laugh on me. Perhaps I wish you to for all my wickedness. No—this is a nonsense. Grace speaks but the truth. I, acting as preacher to myself will tear up my own sermons if I am not careful. It is a simple matter, after all, or one so wondrous that it coils about the limbs and mind with quick desire. Really, I am too much trapped by this and that. "Be clear in your intentions—all shall then obtain." So was taught to me by dear Mama—the very while perhaps that Grace was being upended in a stable. Life is droll indeed. Here is the stream again, my horse refreshed, the sleeking waters frothing to its jaws as surely I shall froth again this night. Perhaps.

Lunch will be ready soon. I shall put such a face upon it as shall disarm all, bring merriment to the table, a casting-down of veils. Orientals, I am told, betray their feelings less than we—upon their cheeks no spider-creep of doubts. Who seeks within my mind shall find a ravaging of thoughts as show not in my eyes. I shall be stern . . . no . . . mild—or yet amusing, not slipping in the ditch of flippancy nor floundering in doubt, but clear in my intentions, yes. Angel or devil, Grace, I know you not, yet know you of my own philosophy, am timourous to find myself so matched yet, cur-like, take some comfort there within as might a laggard leader find himself deep into battle, pressed on by his troops who thought him in the forefront all the time.

Truly there is no accounting for man's fears save that he brings them on himself. Upon my entry, Phillipa looks away and muses on the view, yet has a set contentment in her eyes. Her tapered fingers now have held my prick. She knows the length, the strength, the throb of it as soon enough you shall who sit demure and know yourself enthroned within my mind, I swear.

"Shall you drive with me this evening?" So I ask you when the meal is done. You have neither moved away from me nor to me. Asking you before the others, as I do, there is a safety in it. I have judged that well enough for you. You may refuse, extend uncertainty, or plead the time as set to other things.

"If you wish me to. Do you wish me to?"

Agnes and Phillipa are gone, set to arrangings of the afternoon.

"It would be pleasant. I have a visit to make. The evening will be fair. You are not so often out and about as might be. Yonder to Brenting we will go, spend but an hour and then return. I am minded to meet a fellow on such business as will not dull you—then we may repair to relaxations, conversation, wine."

Confusion in your eyes. I must beware of this, am watchful for relief I would not wish to see and yet in truth Miss Atherton's stern hand has wended you to take your drawers down to my touch, show off your belly, quim, and take my thumb. Are we both hypocrites of like intent? Think you of wine now rather than of cane? I must even so offer avenues of escape for you. I know not why; it must be so. Phillipa has no need of such. My mind is on that matter clear. Silence obtains. I move my hand to yours, beyond the view of servants, to an alcove drawn.

"I have not given you Miss Atherton's report to read. Remiss on my part. I will fetch it now. You may read it in the garden or in your room, as you may wish, and then perhaps return it to my desk."

"Yes."

That dovelike yes. A quickening of my heart, since it comes clear. I have no need to bid you follow me. You do so with a neat submissive air that yet retains an independence in your step. I mark within my errant thoughts your drawers that lie beside the cane beneath the couch still. You, too, have thought of them I know as wistful at my desk you stand and take the papers from my hand. The words therein are not intended for your eyes yet will act as entr'act to the hours betwixt last night and this.

The gesture absolves me. I believe it does. Other voices, other rooms. You may upon the reading of it run and hide, or treat me coldly, blush dismay, yet will not dare to crush a page of it. Thus will I have you caught between guile and purpose—yours and mine I add with sweet hypocrisy—yet leave ajar a door for your escape. Besides in saying *yes* you have said more yeses than you know, might well have demurred and turned away, left me to fret and known not how to handle things.

"If the gentleman is out, his sister will receive us. A pleasant woman, full of pleasure and much given to the pleasing of others, too. You will not mind her company, Elizabeth?"

"No—I will not mind. What shall we speak of? I may be too shy."

"Your shyness lies beneath the couch, my pet."

A blush now tingles to your cheeks. You look away, count fairies in the dust with eyes expressionless.

"I don't know."

"Go to your reading. I would have you read each line of it. The lady will be kind to you tonight."

"The lady?" Now your eyes kingfishers are, darting across the waters of uncertainty. "But I thought. . . ."

"Or take your penance here, my pet. Go read. I so instruct you to. Or must I cane you now?"

"No, please! You said tonight—and now you say tonight that we. . . ."

"Will discourse pleasantly enough—take wine—be at our ease."

I over-speak, of course, too hasty in my explanations and ever a Chinese box of words, one coming up revealing yet another, no doubt have overplayed my part, revealed too much but deem it for the best. No lamb completely to the slaughter you shall ever be, but neither must I deem you far too innocent, I who have made you jiggle to my thumb and brought your tongue to pass between my lips. Grace will not so much manipulate you as us both. Thus is my conscience clear, uncertainties resolved.

"Very well." Oh what a petulant twist you give to your hips in saying that and turning slow away! Minx that you surely are within—as all are save those too dull to take to bed—why do I cast you as cherub?

Yes, the faults are mine entire—I am convinced of it.

"At six fifteen we leave. You will be ready, yes?"

"Yes, very well"—are gone, are gone.

The clock ticks on, The stage is set.

CHAPTER
eight

"A fine coming you had of it on such an evening! Harold is not here—I do regret—was called to business in another shire. May I entertain you both? Elizabeth, is it not? Had you been here this afternoon we might have had a picnic, flourished our skirts upon the lawn and laid thereafter in the long, cool grass. Goodness, what a pretty bonnet! Your gloves as well, my pet—yes, cast them down and let us be at ease. You have not eaten yet? I trust you have not. I have a table set for three and then perhaps we may repair upstairs and take our leisure while the blackbirds sing. I am told that they change their notes and trills from season to season but, alas, have never had the time to notice it. Come, my dears—you'll take a sherry first?"

A rush of words as leaves across the lawn before a wind and then we are within the dining room. I had not expected such preparations, yet they comfort. Smother with words then put to action—maybe that is the trick of it. I do not mind at all, feel utterly at ease. You in a watered-blue and lowcut gown have on our journey here evinced no trepidation though our talk was mundane, sought no corners to evade and trod no prickles. As to Miss Atherton's report, I said nothing of it, saw it not returned though it lay upon my desk again before we left. Better to have left you hedged by question marks, I think. A pox on thinking! Let us to the moment—moments on.

"Do you wear drawers, Elizabeth? I find them fret-some—do you not?"

So suddenly put is the question in the pouring of the sherry that one looks immediately to the answer.

"Often, yes."

You will die, will blush? You stare into your glass.

"Not when inopportune to do so though, I trust? They have coiled about my ankles most when I wished them not there at all. The ladies of Paris, so I hear, are wearing split ones."

"Oh, you can buy them here."

By force of convention, you exchange politenesses, lips tense a little but your eyes not painted yet with indignation. I shall tell you later—if you are in a mood for it,—how my Aunt Miriam was given to the most socially-shocking of remarks and was much feared for it when that which is known as polite company was present.

"How the privy smells!" she might say after having left and then re-entered the room, though this was naught to her utterance one evening when, admittedly slightly in her cups, she drifted in as might a delicate vagrant to declare, "Do not go in the first-floor bathroom yet. I have passed wind there. It must have been the cabbage." Several cases of apoplexy were said to have succeeded this remark, but I doubt it. Rather it would be that a stony silence fell, Mama or Papa coming to the rescue with some jovial remark that indeed the wind was high that night and banging all the shutters. The most grotesque attempts were made to cover up my aunt's remarks, but none succeeded for her voice was exceedingly clear and such prolonged silences as occasionally followed her declarations were said to have been awesome and frequently broken only by Hannah or another jumping up and playing loudly on the piano. Often with dischords, I might add, if their hands were nervous.

I have turned away. It seems better that I should, and mindlessly peruse a view of photographs in silver or in wooden frames. Grace has lowered her voice. I am grateful for that and cannot hear her remarks. There are murmurs from yourself, narrow in tone and rimmed around with caution.

To the table then, I having in mind—as I endeavour to pretend to myself—nothing in particular, discourse on photography, its art and purpose.

"My niece was taken in the nude—a perfect prettiness. I will show you later." This from Grace who would add something else, but I frown at her, comb herring with a fork. Her vitality over-runs her and is not immediate to the moment, yet she still drums on. "It is quite the rage in London—for one's most personal friends, of course. Sir Bertram Abinger—you will have heard of him of course—has a fine apparatus of cherrywood and brass with *the* most elongated lens. He has, to my certain knowledge, taken likenesses of his wife and daughters in a state of Nature. Purely for their boudoirs, so you understand?"

"Indeed yes, Grace, but as to . . . ."

My interruption is in vain.

"Of course, there are photographers who will not direct their art to such matters. Lady Constance Drew, I hear, is one, though does a portrait quite superbly. As to myself, I have been endeavouring to emulate the masters"— so Grace purrs.

"You?"

My astonishment is considerable, genuine. I sense she has a purpose to it all while you, not fallen yet from grace (if I may make so dreadful a pun again) absorb yourself in fish.

"Think you that I am so bereft of talent, Humphrey? Dear Harold himself bought me the photographic apparatus. I will show it to you both upstairs. When we are ready to retreat. We shall be soon. I thought us all to have a light repast that it might not weigh too heavily on our pleasures. Know you anything of the photographer's art, Elizabeth?"

Of course, you shake your head and bite your lip, would look at me but have not quite the courage to. Grace, so I understand, has thrown her line. It floats upon the water close to you, will not be nudged away and has a fly of artless colours and attractions. More wine poured, and then liqueurs. Our lips are burnished by the latter's tingle, bellies warmed by wine and food within.

"Come—we shall go up—have coffee in my room. Humphrey, I shall teach you the fine art that you may practise it."

I know a little of the matter—North lights, roof windows and the like, would say something of the lack of light which here is lambent but not overbright. Grace nudges me and we ascend. There waits us in her drawing room, a small Cyclops, a hooded form from whence a lens peeps out—three brass-encrusted legs of tripod splayed upon the carpet. As I cannot fail to notice, Cyclops has his eye upon the larger of the sofas where silk cushions lounge.

"Elizabeth, undo your dress, if you so please, while I induct him in the art of bringing out a likeness. Humphrey—here—you dip your head beneath this velvet cloth and then through frosted glass, or some such as it is called, perceive the view before you. A plate is already within. You need but to withdraw the silver sheathe, then press this bulb. . . . Elizabeth! You are dressed still!"

"Oh, I—oh!"

Hands to your cheeks you stand and stare, and I am come now to this artfulness of Grace, so take my place upon the platform's breadth—direct the players, as it were.

"It will take but a moment, sweet Elizabeth. I shall join you. Shall I do?"

Grace intervenes before I yet can speak, but it is better

so. I am, as I understand it, still within the wings, cast perhaps as Second Persuader. Best now that I bury my head again beneath the cloth, pretend to fiddle. The view is clear yet to my vague surprise is upside down. A certain piquancy to that, however, since I perceive Grace standing on her head and doffing her fine gown, displaying stockinged legs up to her naked bottom—for she wears naught else (save garters, if you will).

"Oh!"

You are clearly incapable of exclaiming anything else, can scarce be blamed for that but now must follow suit.

"Humphrey—can you see? Close your eyes, you bad man, for I mean to undress her, too."

"No-WOOOOH!"

"Why yes, my dear, stand still—he cannot see. What can he see beneath that big black cloth? Oh, what a silly! Do not struggle so and—yes, Miss—now your drawers as well. Were you not taught so to display? I trust you have been. Humphrey, we are all but ready. Elizabeth, lie down. I will accommodate myself beside you that the likeness may be captured in the instant."

"Are you ready?"

So my voice resounds, a trifle muffled, clear enough to hear, displays apparent ignorance of what portends.

"She will not lie still, the sillikins. May I not have your aid?"

I emerge. The upside-down world is reversed again. A hunted fawn beneath her full rich curves you lie. Her bottom protrudes magnificently, she being half upon you and one stockinged knee thrust up between your own to rub against your fur. Your hands clutch haplessly her arms, wild eyes beseech. I see your nipples yet, the brown thorns offered to my hazing sight.

"Lie still, my pet, it is but a likeness to be taken, then you may be dressed."

"Doo-dooo-dooooh!"

You will not betray it otherwise by speech as now her knee rotates around your slit so slowly, with such measure, that the lips betray their oily pouting to my eyes.

"She will be a good girl. Will you not be, Elizabeth?" Grace coos and lays a kiss upon your awestruck face.

In a sense, I suppose, I see my position usurped. It is not that I feel jealousy; the scene is one of great enchantment. Yet being, as it were, displaced I feel beyond control of things and must regain my rights. As might a doctor to a patient, I kneel behind your head and kiss your ear.

"Bring your lips together that I may take your likenesses so. How pretty that will be!"

"I don't . . . it feels . . . unseemly . . . let me go!"

So you whimper but in muted tone while Grace's hands upon your shoulders rest and hinder you from rising whereupon I bring my murmur to your ear again and let my tongue dip in the shell-like whorl.

"A prettiness it will be, Elizabeth."

A pleading in my voice. It should not be so. I begin for a moment to regret the evening and in my mind rehearse preferred events. There is a looseness here by which I mean untidiness, the interventions of one who was not within my dreams of you and comes as hawker to the door, steps in the kitchen, makes themselves at home.

"It could not be sh . . . sh . . . shown!" you whine and twist about.

"Will you be caned?" Grace hisses down at you, rises a little and her face full puffed.

"She will not be, no. Let her dress. I shall wait downstairs. Elizabeth, you will follow."

The scene is turned about, the comedy all disarranged upon my words which bring a look of disbelief to Grace's face. Indeed, her mouth opens. I note one of her teeth crooked and another black. Her turgid nipples dangle on

your own. I must not, however, afford her time to reply
or all will be undone. I have done such little prompting
as I might, yet even so cannot betray you further.

"Humphrey—wait!"

The voice of Grace pursues, but I am through the door,
noting by absences of sound the servants gone or perhaps
it is the haunting emptiness of air that so informs—a
loneliness of paintings on the wall as I descend, hear
scuffles from above and murmurings.

I surprise myself. Had you but bleated out some petulant remonstrance and Grace with her arts parting your
legs wider, delving her mouth down to your fur—all such
manner of actions, details, whims of moment, postures,
as one can think of—then it might have been other and I
upon you yet or heaving to your bottom's peachlike glory,
peg inserted tingling, deep. Yet came the rapier of your
logic—a thrust I knew not how to avoid nor would not,
could not.

Yes, I do confess there was something tawdry in the
matter. Beyond the ethos, as it were. Miss Atherton would
frown and tap her cane impatiently. I swallow, feel a
nervous thirst and with a sense of guilt as but a guest, go
to the dining room and take some wine, but then regain
my posture in the hall, door open and the evening light
upon me still. Then you descend, your footsteps quick
and I precede you silently. The coachman descends, opens
the door, and you within smooth out your folds of dress.

"What a dreadful woman! I had no idea of it."

"She made me undress."

"I know. I had no seeing of it, thought it but a joke, a
game. That damned enfolding cloth." My voice trails off.
I swallow all the pebbles of my words.

"You asked me to kiss her."

"Did you not understand? I thought it voluntary. All
happened at such speed."

"I suppose, yes. I am thirsty." You swallow, dissolve to

shyness again though whether real or put on for my benefit I do not know.

"We shall stop at an inn, then. There is one at Petford. Jarvis—turn about!" I bellow through the window and sit down again. My legs have brushed your own. You did not stir. "We have no haste." I mutter it a little, turning my intentions upside down like drawers from which all private papers flutter. Snowstorm of indecision, and I lost in it.

"I knew naught about the photographs."

"I saw your surprise." Your voice is prim and yet it cedes to me.

"How proud you were! I had great pride in you, my sweet."

"Did you?" You swallow, gaze at me and turn away, grown as it seems in stature, self-possession, such as makes my pleasure mingle with a certain disappointment that all is not as it was—and that upon my folly with the woman. I lay my hand upon your thigh and feel your stocking top ridge through your dress. Again you do not stir. I move my fingers, feel your skin above.

"Your drawers were pretty—even more so than the ones you left beneath the couch last night."

"They are my new ones."

You do not object to the passing of my hand. Perhaps it soothes you now, your profile to the window set and I the tip of your nose, curve of your lips to savour. Thus we sit, I fondling gently, and we are at Petford soon enough. As you descend, uncertain gaze about, I murmur to the coachman to be gone, return not until ten. You see him go, say nothing, and beside me walk.

"It will be noisy here—the yokels and half-gentry gathered. We may drink outside perhaps and then walk on. You wish to walk a little while?"

"Yes, if you wish."

I am not spurned then. At least I am not spurned. A

tingling in my loins assumes a trust that all is not yet lost
and much may be regained. The fire shall burn again—
it surely shall-though I bereft of cane and some authority.
Quickly enough you take your cider down, aware of male
eyes on your form while I at furtive faces glower or
pretend simply not to have seen them. You wear little
enough in all conscience—a dress, chemise, no under-
skirt. Is it usual for you thus to go about? I ask you as
we walk, though make a joke of it.

"Sometimes. Not really—no. I thought . . . thought if
you changed your mind and meant to cane me . . . did
not know what to do."

"Come down the slope with me—walk through this
wood."

I have your hand. Complicity is ours, or if it is not then
I'll take the wind of it and cast my wagers that the moment's ripe. There is shade and light here now beneath
the trees that stand sufficiently apart to let us wander.
Moist your palm to mine, the exudations of the skin that
fair excite.

"You thought that I would cane you?"

"Said you would." Your voice a mumble, eyes averted
yet.

Against an oak, your back to bark, I place my hands
upon your hips, hold you quiescent so.

"I may spank you even yet. She would have put her
tongue to you tonight."

"I know." Your face suffused and head hangs down.

"As Miss Atherton did? Between your legs after the
birch had burned your bottom sweet?"

You shake your head and crumple into me. My arms
enfold you, hold you tight and feel the roundness of your
breasts to me.

"Under your cunny the flicking of her tongue? Was it
not so? How hot you must have wriggled to her touch
and known the pleasures of it then! Draw up your skirt

and turn about, push out your bottom. You have not told me all. Slowly, my pet, as you were taught."

"Someone may see! Oh, do not spank me here!"

"Shall we have nonsense, then? Must I return you to Miss Atherton's?"

"No, please, I do not wish—oh no!" Snivellings but I disregard them, know them false as you will know I know them false. I glide my hands down your slim back and palpitate your orb, so warm, so ready for the fray the skin's a-tingle to my palms. Grace has performed her magic yet, though not in her own wise. Fretsome and shoulders hunched you turn. I take your hands, limp as they are and place them low against the bark, so forcing you to bend, your bottom thrust towards me, legs apart and toes turned in. You know your postures, as I do observe, and bring your skirt up, fingers tangling to your bows until the close sheathing of your drawers is displaced and the material crumples down, and down and down and down to ankles glides.

Dear orb of sweetness, cleft and apple-round! You snuffle, murmur, make a piteous sound that but persuades a wickedness to me. I know your artfulness, your guile, and dip my fingers underneath your globe to taste the pouting of your nether lips. Ah, how you squirm and hiss your breath out as I do! You would retract your hips indeed, but—SMACK!—my hand adorns your cheeks with pink, and shrilly then you squeal.

"OOOOH-HOOO!"

"That was but a first one, as you know. Come, orb it out to me and stretch your legs apart. No—wait—I'll have your drawers off, Miss. Lift up your heels! Or will you yet be caned as well?"

"D . . . d . . . don't spank me hard!"

"Display yourself! Come, dip your back and let me see your darling quim as well. You were full taught so—this I know." "B . . . but it's wicked—OUCH!"

Another smack, my fingers splayed leave their imprint upon your rearing cheeks and cause it prettily to squirm.

"S . . . s . . . s . . . s . . . ooooh! Someone may see! Ah no! Oh, not so hard!"

"Will you be QUIET! I had no nonsense such as this last night."

"It's d . . . d . . . different then. I mean, we were within and—YOOOOH!"

"Within, without, you'll have it now, my pet"— SMACK! SMACK!—"I'll bring you to obedience yet."

"Boo-HOOOO! I w . . . w . . . was last night. . . . I let you—NEEEE-OOOOH! You p . . . p . . . promised not to sm . . . smack me hard! YAH-HAAAR!" you screech as yet another lands and brings the pink up to a fiery glow.

"Now, my love, my pet, be still," I growl. I know not why I'll not perform the deed with you as yet, but bare my cock and bring it just to thrum against your orb whose heat flares out into my loins. The knob is thrust deep upwards twixt your cheeks at such an angle now as holds you fast by help from my two hands clamped at your hips.

"NOOO-HOOO-HOOOO!" You bubble out your protest, but at my growl you dwindle into silence as my balls couch up beneath your quim and fat are squashed beneath the moist warm lips of you. I brace my legs, so stand, have you at pillage as I wished and feel the ardent burning of your derriere at last pressed to my prick. Now I have thus, it seems, regained my disciplines, those which far-fluttered in my thoughts to match in part your own. How curious! We are as statues bonded into one another, though more vibrant.

"Move your bottom deeper into me, Elizabeth!"

"I c . . . c . . . can't!"

"Come, Miss, you can. Bulb it full in!" I urge my balls up deeper as I speak and feel your lovemouth open, balm of mist that seeps therefrom. You strain and wriggle, tighter to me are, and I in wonder at my strange restraint. My hands slip, glide, and part your cheeks that now expose your nether hole and rub its rubbery ridging to my knob that at an angle's placed to it.

"Thus—so—Elizabeth when I next cane you—yes!"

A gurgled yes from you and we are still, my swollen balls a-churn whose gruel I'll not release yet and so slow step back, trousers a-gaping and my rod full seen the moment that you rise and turn. I'll have you do so now. The game is all but won yet need not be concluded now. My whims have taken a new turn. I know not why nor question it.

"Turn round, Elizabeth, turn round."

I am the master, am I not? Your drawers a-droop, your bottom sparked with fire, a prettiness of stockinged legs, pale thighs and garters tight you lift and turn with flashing naked hips, skirt coiled up still. Open your eyes as open is the sky as my stiff prick comes underneath your view, portraying majesty of veins, full thickness of the stem and bulbous head whose single eye stares up between your own.

You would wilt and falter at the look of it, blush hotter to your brow than ever I have seen. A darting downwards swoop would bring your drawers up, but my gaze forbids. I am Priapus come alive to you.

"Bend. Draw them up slowly. Does your bottom sting still?"

"Yeth." You lisp the yes, inveigling or by accident, perceive as well I know the full hang of my balls, my thickened root, and have the ghost of it pressed to you yet. Not until you are covered do I conceal my stalk, as bitterly as it must be pressed within my trousers where it leans as does a heavy girder to a wall. Order is restored between we two, the balance is reset.

"You will take up your French again, Elizabeth. I would like you to do so."

"If you wish. Yes, if you wish."

We are at formalities again, and yet the dance has changed, has brought its tempo closer to my needs. A hint of dusk intrudes—brings hopeful dark. That I had no need of dark, enchants. Our walk is slow, words measured, nothing said of what has passed, and thus it should be so in my philosophy. I at least did rescue, praise you. Perhaps you took account of that. No matter. One must take the way of all things as they come. "Spit not at the sun—you will not put it out," so Mama often said and thus referred to all inevitables. Papa was the pragmatist—she the philosopher. I doubt that she enjoyed her joustings less. I saw her thighs, legs of her drawers once, might have seen more had I been bold. Perhaps I should tell you so. You would have greater understanding of all then—or would you have? You are new-come to it, will know the richest pleasures of us all. The first cigars I smoked ever tasted better than they do now.

"You were awake last night," I say, and come upon a venture here, a bubble to break, a sail to raise.

"I could not sleep—heard voices as I thought, but it was only you. I saw you pass and knew all well."

"Indeed." The moment of my morning dread is gone. Even though we speak in slow circumference around our inner thoughts it does not matter.

The coachman waits. A knowing fellow who returns a little earlier than told. We accommodate ourselves comfortably. Phillipa waits or waits not, I do not know. Her bottom I might polish with a strap. The thought strikes deep. I may have you both together yet, a-wriggling to the martinet, the cane, the birch. There are no shadows that I can perceive or none that cannot be quick brushed away. Let there be fulsomeness—ripeness is all, as Shakespeare said. My cock stands stiff. The pressure of the hard seat underneath my balls contrives it so and causes it to throb anew.

It is dark in the carriage, your profile illumined now and then by peepings of the moon between the trees.

Agonies of lust have I for you, but if I touched you now the moment would be spoiled. Thus even as I punish you I punish too myself. A newness yes, but I am come to it.

"At eleven in the morning in the summerhouse. You will attend?"

"Yes."

I have asked, have been received.

In thee my field of harvestry shall thrive.

CHAPTER
nine

Phillipa is absent on our return—out, it seems, with Captain Jervis whom I do detest. I swear he wears a corset tighter than her own. Agnes puts on a look of vague discomfort while you, retiring, leave the field of night to me. Tompkins broods over an ailing lamp and then departs, skirt trailing heels, the door closed quiet upon the drawing room.

Phillipa's absence gives diversion from the questions I might otherwise have faced from Agnes who has wondered also at your outing with me.

"If the girl is later than ten-thirty"—so I growl.

"She may dally all the night since you but let her or have done in the past, Humphrey."

"It comes upon me that she needs the birch, my pet."

Thus we play tennis with our words, my wife to serve and I to the defence at first but—veering to the net—take up attack.

"Hah! You have left that rather late, I think. It is ever so with men who put their business first. What a fuss and a squealing she would make, besides. Her age overtakes her in the matter now."

"A curious mood you have on you tonight! I will do my duty, Agnes, and bring her to heel, I promise."

"You have promised such before, my love, and what has come of it? Such sounds of disapproval that you have made before on her late homecomings have stirred her not. Neither have they brought about a mending of her ways. At her age. . . ."

"Bah! She is but twenty-three and might as soon have her drawers scorched as another. That will teach her tricks she never knew before."

"Bravado has you in its spell, I think. I shall to bed, Humphrey, and read. Tompkins will let her in if you retire. I shall admonish her in the morning, if she's late, and do at least my duty that way. I doubt that she will listen, or will merely give pretence to do so."

"Phillipa shall be dealt with, Agnes, but let us have some guile in this. You rightly say that she will fuss and fret or cry out loud upon my disciplining her. That being so, I will attend her in her room when she retires. You will not then interfere, my love?"

"You mean it, then? You do?"

"A minute past ten-thirty and her bottom shall be basted, this I swear. Give no account to such cries as proceed from her."

"Well, we shall see. Provided her sweet face shows penance in the morning, I shall not be displeased. Be not too hard on her, though, Humphrey, but just sufficient."

Rather shall I be hard *in* her, so I vow. Some trick of fate is here that dusts my plans with gold. Never has Agnes spoken so fully in this way before, has shown disgruntlement but no more than that, nor have we spoken of the birch, bottom or bedroom in respect of Phillipa. Such things are frequently accepted, but not said in other households.

"Sleep well, my pet." Agnes rises and we kiss. A rare event. We seldom kiss goodnight, being gone to our own

ways latterly, she to her comforts and I to thoughts of
disciplines I now would fathom deeper. Her mouth comes
lustrous to my own—echoes of follies once performed
when we were younger, frotting on a rug as soon as on a
bed. I palm her bottom, large as a full moon, and would
in this moment have at its plenitude as willing as at
Phillipa's.

"Let not Elizabeth be disturbed, Humphrey, if you are
to stay up for Phillipa's return."

"I shall so try. You had best warn her, though, in passing up to bed."

"Perhaps, yes. You think it wise? I do not know. A
mention perhaps. The merest. One must not alarm her—
she is always good."

"Indubitably—and yet a quick-thrown word? Best that
she knows the reason for Phillipa's cries, if such there
are to be. I leave it all to you in this respect. Sleep well
and stir not. All shall be well. The dear girl may return
in but an hour or so, and then no need for these alarms."

"Of course. I am sure she may. Even so. . . ."

Agnes drifts out, embroidery abandoned. How very
odd—how odd indeed—that events should come together in this way. *"Even so. . . ."* What did she mean
by that? Women have a trick with words that I have often
envied, leaving them as biscuits on a plate that one may
toy with, nibble afterwards, and yet not truly find the
flavour of nor know why they were left.

I discard my jacket, remove my cravat. A faint mum-
bling of voices from above that pleases, stirs, excites. In
a curious way I do not want to know what is being said.
Agnes will surely wear a solemn look. Do I betray you
thus? Will you envisage it already—feel a tinge of jealousy? I hear your door close first, then hers.

"Do you wish me to stay up, sir?"

Tompkins has entered—longs for bed, I'm sure. Of
course, in such a mood as I am now, bull pawing at the
gate, I take more note of her in masculine ways. Some

gentry are giving to disciplining their maidservants as well. The girls accept it rather than be put out, so I have heard.

"You may pour me a whisky first and then retire."

Her face at least has a placid look, not over-tired nor eager but accepting duties as part of her rote of life. She must turn to the sideboard now and bend. I wish her to. Grey stockings that I care not for, but a nice turn of ankle and a glimpse of calves, a bottom well-moulded, neither sparse nor over-plump. I cannot help myself—a tenseness of over-excitement, no doubt. Visions of you bending at the tree. How strange is Time that events, so close upon this hour or that, displace themselves so rapidly, leaving behind but images as upon a photographic plate.

"Did Miss Phillipa say at what time she would return?"

I come closer upon the girl, glass placed, decanter in her hand, and stand behind her.

"No, sir, but she never says nothing of such things to me. Went off with Captain Jervis, she did, an hour or more past."

"I know. You may take a glass also, Tompkins. It will help bring sleep easier to you."

"I, sir?" Her astonishment is great. The whisky poured, she stands uncertain. Servants are given to filching tipples when they can. I am not such a one who has ever marked the level of wines, spirits, liqueurs, in bottles, as some masters do, nor weigh the meats nor count the loaves. I cannot resist the moment, take her wrist and guide her hand down to another glass upon the shelf below.

"I'm sure you have worked hard today, Tompkins, and deserve it."

"I have sir at that, but Mistress don't allow. . . ."

"She is to bed. Come, let me fill your glass. Do you take to spirits?"

"I do, sir, yes—a little I do. Oh, you squash me!"

I do indeed. In reaching around to the front of her my hand brushes breasts that I find pleasingly firm, her bottom is bulbed in to my loins. A hot flush on her neck. She stirs, but knows not how to move or if to move, must feel the rising of my cock and I—knowing that I am at a madness here—am dizzied with images I cannot well dissolve no more than one in a storm can brush the winds away.

The sound of liquid poured into a glass—a glugging of satisfaction in its release. My hand is steady at the least, knuckles contriving to erect her nipples.

"If the Mistress come, sir . . ."

"She will not my dear. Let us drink as friends do. Hand me my glass across your shoulder—so. Now take up yours and turn and link your arm around mine so that we may drink with wrists crossed."

"I shall spill mine when I turn, sir."

"No, you won't. There—slowly, slowly. You see? It is achieved."

Belly to mine. Her thighs to mine. My penis pounding in between our clothes and forearms locked one up against the other. Her face a-fluster, eyes impounded by uncertainty.

"The Mistress does not come down, Tompkins, once abed."

"I know, sir. Miss Phillipa might arrive. She'll think it strange. Oh, sir!"

My free hand delves between us, finds her skirt and draws it up until her thighs are bared. How warm and moist she is between—what richness here! Twist of my wrist and gliding of my fingers to her fur. Plumpness and curls and full rolled lips.

"Open your legs, my dear, and drink your drink."

"Sir, I never. . . . WOOOOOH!"

My fingertip the lovelips part. Her head hangs back and glass a-wobble, bottom pressed into the sideboard's front.

"Open them, Tompkins! Mabel, is it not? Do as your master bids! By heaven, what gorgeous thighs you have!"

"I c . . . c . . . can't drink like this, sir."

"Take hold of something then, my dear. Bring your hand down—unbutton me—and fetch it out. You've felt a prick before, I'm sure."

"I sh . . . sh . . . shouldn't sir!"

"There! Is it not big enough for you? My god, let me get it under, up beneath your cunt the while we drink. Is this not a fair game? Frot your belly to mine. Is this not nice?"

"Oooo-wer! Oh, you make me feel funny, sir!"

"But nice? You see, you have drunk quite a bit in your excitement."

"I'll sp . . . sp . . . spill it if I'm not careful."

"I, too, if you but work your belly faster, girl."

My nut slips back and forth beneath her lips which are as moist as a cut peach. A well-furred and wholesome quim she has—ripe for the game. Glasses a-spill, our arms unlocked, I embrace her, bring her mouth to mine, our knees a-quiver, cup her bare bottom fervently. A-gobble-gobble go our mouths, hers partly open, lustful to my tongue.

"Have you been birched yet, strapped, put to the cane, Mabel?"

"Nooo-hoo-hoo sir! Oh, don't put it in!"

"You hold your legs wide, girl, as you should. Let me feel your bottomhole. Has it been breached yet? What a delicious rim!"

"Nooo-hooo, it's bad! You're naughty with me, stop! NA-HAAAAR!" She wriggles fore and aft, quim to my cock—though I embed it not—and hot cheeks to my finger's dipping-in, moans fretfully and twists her mouth about. "Do-hoh-on't!" she gurgles, grips my shoulders tight.

I am at madness here and know it. I have descended to the pits of crudity, am reading the wrong lines, have taken a lesser actor's part, and all for lust, and all for lust. Better that my entertainments were kept quiet, not spread abroad, displayed to all the world. Even so, the girl is more attractive than I thought, has a delicious mouth, is fit to kiss and frot with. I would encounter Phillipa in my stallion-state, and not as one whose prick is floppy with remorse.

"Disobedience does not become you, Mabel."

I affect a new tone—draw my finger out from twixt her bottom cheeks, step back and show my penis to her full, not in bravado but with casualness.

"You . . . you come upon me so sudden, sir." Mouth open, face a little puffy, still attractive, though.

"I may come upon you as suddenly with a tawse, my dear. Hold your skirt up still—do you hear?"

"It's rude, sir, standing like this, sir."

Her left inner thigh has a small mole upon it, as a beauty spot, her garters tawdry, stocking tops tucked in and too much wrinkled for display. A fine bush she has, well curved beneath her mount. Her legs tremble and she makes to close them. A quick smack, she squeals, and stands awry.

"That is better, Mabel. Let it fall now, smooth it down. A splendid pair of legs you have, my girl, and nicely bulbing bottom. Have you not been praised before?"

She knows not whether to laugh or cry, has wonder in her eyes. I tuck my prick away and let it pulse beneath my shirt. Twice have I done so now tonight and wonder at it. Lips quiver, but she cannot bring reply.

"Have you not? Has it not been smacked and made to glow, my girl?"

"A bit, sir, afore I come into service yet, when Dad were strict with me. I didn't like it, though."

"Too harsh? Too harsh was he? You minded not obedience then, perhaps. Another drink, then, and you may to bed."

"I dunno if I want, sir."

"Yes, you do. Fill both and bring them. We shall easy

stand. You'll not raise your skirt again tonight, but on the morrow may. You understand?"

"If you say, sir. But I don't want to do it rude."

What simpleness of mind is here! Better your subtleties, my sweet, if such you have, or else I conjure them myself within your mind. Her step uncertain, whisky poured anew, the maid slow comes to me. I have stepped further back, arranged myself of a purpose on the carpet's spread that she might learn a particular submissiveness of approach to me. Such detail is important and I must not fumble it whatever the appeal of her. I may after all add to the harem. Such a bizarre thought strikes, amuses. Cock of the walk I stand, am conscious of it, fuzzed for a moment with a self-importance that I would cast off but nets me close. Of course, with a servant it is different. So I tell myself. I have not wandered in these woods before, not counted each tree as my own.

"What is rude, Mabel?"

"Dunno, sir."

"You have shown your bottom when you have been spanked, have you not?"

"Was made to, sir, yes."

"Have held a cock and frotted it, I'm sure. Afterwards, afterwards? Have you not afterwards?"

"It was rude, sir."

"Well, you did at least. Such is a sign of advancement in you as it is in all young ladies, for a young lady you be even though you are a servant. Is it not nice to think so?"

"Nobody ever called me that before, sir."

She cannot help but smile, looks pleased. I shall have her yet. She knows it well.

"Then I so do, my dear. Now, drink your whisky. Let it warm within and then you may to bed."

Our drinking is reflective, slow—she preferring silence, I enjoying it. I have donated her a phrase that swims still in her mind. That she is a "young lady" is a newness to her. Perhaps after all I caught the moment well—need not admonish myself too much for hastiness. Her waist is slim. I mark it so by running one hand all about her hips, into the curve and down again. She breathes a little faster—does not stir. The servants at Miss Atherton's are such and put to gentry of occasion while the latter watch their nieces', wards' or daughters' bottoms stirring to the cane through such a peephole as I did enjoy. No sounds stir. I am grateful for it. Phillipa's carriage does not yet arrive. The moment builds, the moment builds.

"Be mindful of what I have told you, Mabel."

"Yes, sir, I will."

I little mutinous, but she is closer drawn. I feel her belly warm again to mine and let my prick throb to its curve. Perhaps I should deal with her as I have with you—mix gentleness with quiet commands. The role of martinet, strict as it is and well becoming others, does not suit me. Hannah always laughed and turned away, scorning my youth and inexperience, or used me as a mannikin to tease. She little knows my newfound stature now. I may employ it on her yet, bring her to rippling laughter of amusement, admiration, as I ream her bottom. Two years and I have not seen her now. Pleasant the surprise that awaits her, if the chance obtains. I must set first my own house in order, though, attain the pinnacle first and then survey the valleys broad.

"You will stand so when I wish it, Mabel?"

"Sir?"

"And with your bottom bared, if so I wish. You understand?"

"Yes, sir, but if there's others about. . . ."

"If so I wish. You understand? There will be discretion ever, Mabel."

She nods, head sunk and at the carpet stares. How frequently they do that, minds a-muddle! I take her empty

glass in token that we are as equals in this moment now—
may tip her this way, that, as might amuse me—which
is to say to an excited apprehension or to fulfilment. That
she has been corked already I now little doubt and yet is
minded to evade the penis-probe as many do till they are
brought to better knowing of it.

"Go to bed, my dear. Do you lock your door?"

"No, sir, I ain't got no key. OOOOH!"

My fingers dip between her cheeks that bulb beneath
the covering of her skirt. She grits her teeth, strains up
and then sinks down, shoulders a-quiver, pink flush in
her cheeks. I dare to think that she has entertained a
throbbing cock there once or twice, but fancy ever takes
me in this wise. Through the material I feel her puckered
rose then let my hand slink slowly down to cup one cheek
and then another. A pat on both and she is half prepared.

Doubtful she goes. Another mind has now encom-
passed hers. An outerness has come upon her. I, the
villain, hero, of the piece have made her stir my wand.
Its flesh will pulse against her fingers in her night-hazed
thoughts.

Of course, I feel certain tremors, intimations of uncertainty that she might to others speak—a giggling in the
hall, the linen room, a whispering between the shufflings
of the clinker from the grates or emptying of bedroom
bowls at morning, nudge of elbows, faces re-arranged to
meet the Master or the Mistress. Perhaps I should have
slipped a sovereign in her hand, but that is not my way.
She may wait—so I tell myself—in hope of such reward
or, on the other hand, fear of dismissal if she speaks.
Damn me, if that wretched Jervis is at Phillipa. . . . The
very thought invades my balls. A tremulousness of waiting hangs cloud-like above. Warm she'll come and ready
for the sport, but I must not alarm her—would not—nor
do I dare collude and have her privy to my talk with
Agnes. Subtlety must be my passport yet.

CHAPTER

ten

At last a carriage sounds—at last—and by heavens close to midnight, too. I have some reason now for ire, at least, and throw the front door open to her coming. A unique event, I might say. One does not open doors that servants can. Pearls dance about her neck—her bodice so low cut that I might pass my hand within and feel her tits as that damned Jervis has, no doubt.

"Get within!"

"What? Eh?"

"You are late, my love, yet late again. Come upstairs quickly."

"Yooooh! You're hurting me! No, don't!"

Well is her voice heard and our scuffling feet as I would have them be. Your bottom, warm and scented in half sleep, will stir upon your sheet, I know, envisaging in cloudy wonder all you hear. Curl up and close your eyes anew. Imagine yet again my cock against your bottom as it was, unspermed as you still are. I have no doubt the words of that report dance in your mind.

"Into your room, Phillipa!"

"NEEE-OOOH!" The comedy is played although she knows it not, my hand clamped to the nape of her smooth

100

neck. Dark of the room and on the bed thrust down.
Before she can rise I have her skirt full up, rolled on her
belly and her legs hang down, full gartered, frilly legs of
drawers, wonder of white and black, allure of flesh.

All is prepared: that's half the trick of it. Indeed her
hand has already touched the strap I have laid ready for
her on the bed.

"Wh . . . what are you do . . . doing? They'll have
heard!"

"Be quiet!" I have no recourse for it but to growl the
words and keep her pinned while ruffling down her drawers.

"I do-ho-want to! THOOOOOOO!"

Ah, the crack of that broad leather on her gleaming
bum! So agile does she twist and churn that I'd soon as
cork her as give her another, but I swear that Agnes has
her ears at twitch. SCRA-AAAACK! Bark's louder than
it's bite, I know. She'll feel the sting of it, the searing
flame, warm as she is, her flesh refulgent, glowing from
the night. At her first trials too, by Jove, she is. The
thought warms through and gives my arm more strength,
though twist of the wrist is more to the point of it to bring
the leather flat down on the cheeks. Even in the gloom I
watch them squeeze.

"THEEEE-OOOOH!" her cry rings out as down it splats
and brings a pink glow to her ardent orb, my knee upon
the small of her back and she held down as butterflies are
pinned.

Have you heard? My dearest, have you heard how
sounds another to the scorching heat? Curl up as you
may, it will come to you again. Such fantasies return to
me anew that I would have you bending over together,
hip to hip and bottoms orbed in your submissions.

"NA-HAH-HAAAAAR!" Phillipa sobs now truly. Have
I hurt her so, or is it all theatricals? She has bounced this
bottom on a carriage seat this night to other ends—I have
no doubt of it. The thought allays my tenderness, brings

me to splat her twice and thrice again the while she churns it all about and rubs her furred quim on the quilt.

I feel her bottom furtively—hot as it is, and silky is its gloss, squirming as does a fish within the hand. I shall have her in the meadow yet. A fancy takes me to, beneath the sun, wine at our lips, her nipples ravaged, peaking to my lips—while you . . . would you watch such desecration of desire, balls smacking up beneath her cheeks, grass tickling at her cunny as I ream her?

Four, five or six I have awarded her? It matters not. Another and she will be ready for the long thrust of my penis in her nest. Such discipline becomes her on this night, for she might think me prey to her, not conqueror, who comes to lie between her thighs and offer longing groans into her ears. Tamed she has been, but must be tamed the more.

"Why are you . . . why are you . . . yah-hooooo!"

The leather's seared her split globe once again, her darling hips that dance, one leg half raised to offer up her fig to my blurred eyes that mayhap Jervis has already spurted in this selfsame night. Once more—once more— I can scarce stop myself. It is not as with you—not as with you. I know Phillipa well—believe I do. She comes much riper to the fray, needs harder riding, knows it well.

"Don't do it to me-heee-me! NEEEE-YNGGGGG!" The crack that sounds—the loudest yet—sounds through the room. Her bottom hot rotates and now I know her fit for a cooling draught, prod of the penis sinking in or up until she knows the snugging of my balls to her warm flesh. "It may be for the good if she is put to it when crying softly. Such tears are often prelude to the urging of Priapus"—so Miss Atherton did write. Have you well marked such passages or let them skim across your mind and disappear into infinity?

Phillipa's face is covered. Does she really cry? Shall I drink pearls of salt upon her cheeks the while I put her to my cock again? I would not have her cry in such despair as her sobs mean to sound or would convey. Slippery and hot her bottom churns beneath my seeking hand, the strap cast down. My fingers fumble at my trousers now. "Be quick upon it ever the first time—but slower to the second and the third," so your mentor wrote, "for once she has absorbed the manly juice, she'll know its comforting, will wilt and squirm, but still will take it in."

Upon her fourth creaming now is Phillipa. She gurgles, sobs, twists coverlet in wildly-groping hands, but twists her body not away from me.

"Straighten your legs and thrust your bottom up, Phillipa. Do it, or you'll take the strap again."

"OH-WOH! It hurt, it hurt, it hurt!"

My prick half out, a rattling at the door. "Humphrey! Enough, my dear, enough! Come to me, come, and let her sleep."

"I said she'd hear! Oh god!" Upon the bed Phillipa is about now, wincing, thrusting skirt down, legs tangled in her drawers and all awry. All silence comes from you and you alone behind your further door. I open Phillipa's, and Agnes in her nightgown stands.

"My dear!" A stupid utterance and yet I contrive such a faint crack in my voice as makes it seem my own despair matches Phillipa's.

"Come to me, Humphrey, come."

I have not the like of such a situation in my fancies as Agnes turns and with self-conscious daintiness makes for her room, her bottom cheeks a-wobble 'neath her thinly-veiling garment of the night and—with such desperation as I feel—my cock full rigid through my trousers' gap, sprung as an unleashed coil and quivering at the swollen nut.

To pass your door is agony, yet I must. You will not peep tonight and I—not knowing Agnes's true mood—can only follow at a venture. In the room is total darkness, in the room, thank god for total darkness in the room lest my full lewdness be unveiled to her.

"Come, dearest, take your trousers off. Come to me— let me take my nightgown off. The poor girl—how she cried and sobbed and yet there must be discipline."

"There must be, Agnes, yes." My voice is thick. The play is disarranged, yet in a flash is rewritten in this startling wise. I had not allowed for this—not allowed for this at all. In truth I would have mounted Phillipa quickly, spermed her deep, then sought forgiveness tongue to tongue and cozened her with words, skin moist with tears.

How long it is, or seems, since I saw Agnes thus— full-breasted as she is and naked in the gloom. My trousers off, I tear at shirt and socks—have naught else now to do but fling myself beside her. Cock pulsing to her hip we lie in silence, my arm across her belly thrown.

"It was necessary, Humphrey."

"Yes, my dear."

Hand gliding down I feel her fur and hear her sigh. Moistness is there—a fullness—rich between plump thighs that know not fat but a proud firmness still obtain. Her hand moves, gropes, and coils around my prick. Faint quivering of naked forms. An owl hoots, bats fly. All is still, the forest closing upon the travellers who have strayed too deep within.

"Give it to me—give it to me—oh, so long!"

"My darling!"

"Humphrey! HAAAAAR! Oh, get it in! Dear heart, you have not fucked me for so long."

"My dear, I thought, I thought. . . ."

Her legs splay wide and knees bend up, receiving me deep in her lovemouth's clasp. So fervent are we for the fray that it sinks in unhindered at one glide, her thick curls rubbing, rasping, to my own, the tight and jellied mouth that sucks me in, her nipples rubbery and stiff, tongue lapping greedy to my own. Ah, sweet the sting of nestling in a fervent cunt that yet can grip as tightly as a girl's!

"You took . . . took . . . took her drawers down—
AH! Don't move it yet!"

"My love, forgive me. In the moment of my ire with
her. . . ."

"So stiff she made you. Do me—do me slow."

Rushing of breath from her nostrils to my own, her
spurring nipples to my chest and legs wound strongly up
to clasp my waist.

"Agnes, forgive me, if I. . . ."

"Fuck me, darling, fuck." Full squelch of us between
our thighs, knob urging out, knob gliding in. Smack of
my balls up to her urging cheeks. I, trapped and netted,
praised, admonished, scorned or used by her—I know
not. "Her hips they twisted, bottom burning, Humphrey,
yes? What a derriere she has, delicious for her age. You
spurred her on, my pet, I trust?"

"And shall do so again, Agnes, if you but allow."

"T . . . t . . . taking her drawers down, you naughty
thing—oooh-WAH! Go in me faster—faster—fast. If
she is bad again, of course you must, for badness is as
badness does to bring your prick up so."

How abandoned she is! I have never known her in a
like mood such as now. Words babble from her lips as I
would have thought her shamed to speak. My finger
moistened from our rubbing parts, I seek her bottomhole
and urge it up, feeling her grip upon it like a baby's
mouth.

"N . . . naughty Phillipa," she stammers, tongue a-
lashing round my own.

"It st . . . st . . . stirs the senses, pet, I do confess, but
discipline must be maintained henceforth upstairs and
down."

"Whooooo! Humphrey—AAAARGH! You make me
come again!"

In truth she does and soaks my balls, choking her sobs
of pleasure to my mouth as from my stallion-stem the
sperm erupts, floods into her and causes us to cling in

deep-down quiverings of bliss till all is done, her cunny
squeezing on my tool as ardently as yours shall do. All
banners flying now I sink upon her and whisper my praises
in her ears till then, slip-slipping from her, I uncork. The
night is all undone and yet remade. Brushing the fur of
her with my wet knob, I roll aside, then gather her to
face me which she slumbrous does. One pointed nipple
at my bicep rubs.

"I said . . . oh, what I said! Forgive me, Humphrey!"

"You said well as you said, Agnes, yet perhaps must
be admonished for your cries. In amourous combat much
is said, but as to taking down Phillipa's drawers and my
cock being stiff. . . ."

"I know, I know—I pray you will forgive."

"We shall see. You must to penance come as well,
perhaps."

"I will nought say upon the matter, Humphrey, I promise. Did . . . did she struggle much at first? I wondered
only, for I heard her cries."

"One must ignore such cries when discipline is nigh,
my dear. You understood this well tonight, yet entered
on the moment all too soon. Her bottom, warm and
round, was quickly bared, drawers to her ankles and her
skirt full up that she might bulb it better up to me. At the
fourth stroke I cupped her cheeks and held her thus that
she might better understand the posture."

In so speaking I have parted Agnes's plump cheeks,
explored the crevice, toyed with her rosette and dipped
my finger up to the first joint. Breath hissing out, she
straightens down her legs then draws them up again,
knees nudged to mine. I have not held her thus before in
all the years and bring her new to it. Her eyes are lanterns
in the dark. She would cry out, yet knows not what to
say. I silence hold, brush back her hair and kiss her brow.

"D . . . d . . . did you hold her thus, Humphrey?" Her
voice wheedles, is constrained, has a timidity that pleases.

"Were one of them to wriggle hard, avoid the strap,

the birch, the cane, how otherwise might she be held? Extend your tongue, Agnes. Let but the tip of it touch mine."

"H . . . H . . . Humphrey!"

"Will you, too, be strapped, my love? It may be necessary. Do it, now!"

She gulps, extends her tongue, as I do mine and point to point they quiver, not being allowed to slip-slide, glide, or intertwine, but only thus to touch. It is a pleasantry I teach myself. My finger works a little in her bottom's hole, brings her to tremor so that she must clutch with febrile grasp upon my shoulders.

"Excellent, my love—continue the exercise. Let it thus be delicate and sweet. Thus is constrainment showed—no mutinies allowed. Some call it exercising—others, discipline. A maiden is thus taught obedience. I shall fondle now your tits the while I work your bottom to my touch. How hard your nipples are, how firm your gourds! You are as tight as she, my pet. But keep your tongue out straight and jiggle your hips. It sinks a little further up you so, and must do so that you might know your bottom's held, and held to my command."

"HOOOOO! But you have never. . . ."

"Be quiet, my darling. Severity and tenderness combine. You would not have me too harsh be? Come, Agnes, work more rhythmically!"

"You d . . . d . . . d. . . . Oh, Humphrey, I am coming, love!"

"Shush, darling, shush—it ever thus must be. Let me cup your cunt now, feel it sprinkle. Ah! Pulse out your pleasure—rub my cock now fast."

"Oh, dearest, naughty one, you shame, excite!"

"Excitement comes from within you, Agnes. I do but discipline, bring on, ameliorate the stinging of the birch, the cane, the strap, yet let the burning still remain."

"B . . . but with Phillipa. . . . Hoooo! I am coming yet again!"

In truth she does, her stickiness apparent, trickling down my fingers quick and belly all a-shimmer with desire. Now mouth to mouth our tongues exude their fire. My cock upstanding to her belly thrums, then falls her head back and she's done. Slow I uncork her, let my fingertip work up and down her groove and then withdraw. Upon her back she rolls and at the ceiling blindly stares.

"H . . . Humphrey. . . ."

"Be quiet, my love, and your obedience absorb as all must now, though you have not had the strap and so have felt but half of it."

"You will not strap me, Humphrey—pray say not!"

"You have confessed to shame, my sweet. Is that not reason for it?"

"But I said . . . you said . . ."

"IS it not?"

"Suppose—yes, I suppose. And Phillipa? And . . ."

"Discipline is requisite for all. Did you not say so yourself tonight of Phillipa and did she not receive? Make not too much of it. An exercise for all but once a week will, I am sure, suffice. I bid you sleep now, Agnes. Think on it. I have not doused the lamps downstairs. Will then to bed myself. Sleep well. Be comforted in your obedience now. Tomorrow if I bring you to it, raise your bottom proudly as did Phillipa."

"You have not spoken thus before nor ever acted so."

"When did you last ask to be fucked, my sweet? When did you come so much before?"

"Oh, Humphrey!" Rolls beneath the clothes and hides her head—the best of signs. I bend to stroke emerging hair and feel her quiver. "Sh . . . shall you strap me, Humphrey—oh!"

"Tomorrow, Agnes, you will wear no drawers. Nor may the others on my whim. Is this clear understood?"

"Yes, Humphrey, yes, but if. . . ."

"There are no *ifs* nor *buts* nor *maybe's* now. You, too,

may learn to wield the cane yourself upon recalcitrants. Such housemaids as are slovenly perhaps."

"I d . . . do not think I could."

"You will, my dear. The sight of quick-bared bottoms brings desire to sting and make the hips squirm willingly, as soon enough they shall. Though I am Master here, you still are Mistress, too."

"Yes, Humphrey."

"Sleep the sleep of angels, then. Bear all in mind. Though I am changeling come, I am not quite alone in this. Goodnight."

A muffled whisper from her and I'm gone, engaging darkness all about me now. I would to Phillipa, but cannot now explain this contretemps. She must rest, alas, in her uncertainty. To sow some sweet confusion brings advantage to the cause, as well enough I know with you who now to darkling dreams have gone. Naked I descend. The conqueror is come, the vanquished lie in waiting for the prick's arising. Indeed, it upstands now. I have obtained a fiercer virility than I have known before. To stand in one's own drawing room in the dark, naked and erect as I do now, is quite obscene, exciting, strange, awhile the silence hums above.

I may—in drawing back the curtains, peering into dark—just see the hexagonal of the summerhouse from here. The low branch of a tree bisects its top. The cane will thus bisect your derriere. On the morrow—on the morrow.

CHAPTER
eleven

"Stand so, my love. We are come upon a better understanding of the matter, are we not?"

Your derriere comes fervent, silky to my touch, the chubby cheeks full rounded to my palm which up beneath your skirt has groped, blue silk upon my forearm looped in folds. I sit, you stand. So it should be for the moment, for the moment only, your left hand placed uncertainly on my shoulder and your eyes cast down.

The summerhouse is burnished by the sun at morn, but I have drawn the curtains to and cast a lambent light on all. Well-furnished as it is, we have a fine room for such comfortings, with sofa, table, bed, two chairs, a cabinet for wine, a carpet on the stiff-planked floor, an idling rug of tiger skin.

My Uncle Bertram had one such as well. A tennis court adjoined. How well I remember the net at lazy dip and trees around—a horse in the paddock close by and maids who came in their trim uniforms with lemonade, chilled wine, biscuits to nibble and small cakes to flirt with. My uncle in white shirt, white trousers, floppy hat, would command all. Those at the low-pole barrier around the court would watch the foursomes at their springing, jumping, laughter, with gay calls of "Missed! I saw you miss! You hit the line!"

Worst was to hit the net not once but twice in fumbled succession. I refer to the errors of the girls, of course, handpicked as strawberries are and sweet as strawberries would their cheeks be flushed each time a double fault was called. "Go to the summerhouse!" was then the cry. Spectators clapped, though there were few enough, for all who came were brought to play in turn—such was the rule—and never more than a dozen did I count in all.

I was but thirteen then, perched in an apple tree, the lone one who would not be called and none took note of me—thought me too young to understand, though my aunt would tut, look up at me and then look quickly down, pretend to busyness or go indoors as one by one the erring girls were led within the summerhouse and the door closed.

How heady was the scent of apples round my head! Uncle Bertram alone accompanied the girls within. I doubt that he other than smacked their bottoms, warm as their drawers were from their exercise. The presence of my aunt no doubt inhibited him. He would emerge as flushed as they, feeling their bottoms as they went, and they to wait their turn again, for in the interval another girl would have replaced them on the court. I have often wondered about my aunt—whether she enjoyed it or did not. She never played. All who did were younger, and she said the exercise was far too much for her.

The fragments of such scenes as then I saw return and gather into patterns, hazed by summer's perfumes, honey, milk and new-mown grass, lie of the land and bottoms, thighs envisaged. Once I recall a girl who would not play as she was meant to and at her double hitting of the net ran all about as does a rabbit broken from its hutch or stirred at morning by the panting dogs. On seeing her, chased as she was, my aunt retired. I recall clearly seeing the tip of her nose beneath her bonnet as she passed

beneath the apple tree. She always stood alone, apart—
a haunting figure at the feast, as might be said. Behind,
beyond her, sounded cries, high laughter and encourage-
ments as the girl's waist was seized. Her legs kicked high
as, lifted by two gentlemen, she was carried to the summerhouse where Uncle Bertram waited by the door.

"No, please! No! Let me down!" So rang her cries,
assailed the silent treetops, and my aunt was gone into
her hitherness inside the house.

I turned upon the branch and saw my aunt peep—the
tip of her nose at windowpane from within the sheltering
morning room, bonnet a-tilt behind the curtains' hang—
then turned anew and watched the girl bundled as though
by Sabine rape into the summerhouse. I heard the smacks
then—hard they must have been—and knew all four to
be inside. Then my uncle, conscious of his watching wife
no doubt, emerged and stood as nonchalant as he might
upon the steps.

The two gentlemen did not follow suit, nor did the girl
whose squealings could be heard, but fainter, muffled. A
full half hour obtained before all reappeared, though the
game meanwhile proceeded, voices tinkling, rising, falling, thrown like high notes, low notes, to the sun.

I had some youthful fear for the girl, I do confess,
envisaged her as coming out bedraggled, weeping, tear-
ful, all put out, and I the only watcher for the others
always turned their backs upon such merriments, as they
were called, this being always the most tactful custom.
Thus when the green door opened once more, it was to
me as a curtain rising on some awesome revelation at a
pantomime when villains brood within a smoky, greenlit
scene. I had then no ideas of fucking, or very few, and
thought but of retribution such as came to me in the form
of smacks I occasionally received myself from dear Mama.
One gentleman emerged then and I glimpsed behind him
the figure of the girl whose head was lain upon the other's
shoulder. They kissed, to my astonishment, and then

emerged to fair-faint cheers that made pretence to spur the tennis players on. Thus was initiation close upon me, but I knew it not and dwelt in halls of innocence.

I should do so now perhaps and let you so remain. You twitter as I find your rose deep-nestled in between your bottom cheeks, but spread your ankles, are obedient.

"In your report 'twas said that you might disrobe or not for discipline, Elizabeth."

"I know."

Your breath puffs out. I have my finger in your bottom-hole, though just the tip of it to keep you steady, on your toes.

"Disrobe now. I would have it so. Down to your stockings, shoes, and bend. Thrust up your bottom well and legs apart, as you were in her study several times, I vow. Was it not so?"

You do not answer—of a sudden burst away and to the window run that frames your head in its small compassing. Halo of light about your hair, new-washed, that frizzes slightly.

"I d . . . did undress. I do not wish to now."

"You do not wish?"

I am amused at first—believe myself to be—but to amusement anger hinges: feelings that become me not. Your back's to me—your profile hid.

"You will *not* be caned, Elizabeth? Will not?"

Still no reply. I move to you, touch at your shoulders lightly, turn you around. Most girlishly your face comes to my chest, nose poking at my shirtfront. I, the eagle, thus enfold the young, soft-breasted thrush.

"I hate the cane. It stings me so. Once when I caned a girl she cried."

"You caned? YOU caned?" I am off balance, must recover poise.

"Miss Atherton said we must—to see the postures as they would be seen."

"Of course, I had forgotten." *Lies*. My cock in surging

tingle now erupts and stems full up between us as we stand. You will surely feel its ridging through my trousers and your skirt. "You did not mind? How often did you cane?"

"Twice . . . no . . . three times. Lord Brearley's daughter was the worst. She wriggled madly all the time."

"As you do." I permit myself a smile that floats down-like upon your hair.

"No, I don't. Not much. Do I?"

"Divinely so you do. Come, let us talk of this. Sit with me on the sofa. Did you like to cane or birch or strap as well as to receive?"

"Oh, I don't know. Sometimes I did. You should not make me speak of it. Miss Atherton. . . ."

"My pet, she is not here. Your tongue is loosened, let it wag the more. There comes no harm from it that we might speak. You have no cause to tremble with me now. I promise not to cane you if you speak."

"You do? Oh, though, what are you at?"

"Loosen your bodice, dear. Come, let me see your tits and then a truce upon it. Offer your nipples to my fingers while we kiss. What beauties—firm and round and full, my sweet!"

"You make me breathless, shouldn't, no. You said . . . you said . . . to talk. You make me swimmy feeling me like this."

Lustrous your globes and firm as jellied mounds. I bend to suck a nipple, make you start. Its tip is stiff, and fire upon my tongue. Lifting your face, I draw your tongue full in my mouth but then you jerk away. My hand becomes a soothing cup, first underneath one tit and then the other. Moody you look when I would have you amorous, and I in thrall when I should be a-caning you, delighting in your squeals, sight of your quim, your bottom flushed and streaked, rotating—all such as are the condiments of love.

I soothe you, feel your nipples burr, one arm around your shoulders slung, though not so tight as to disturb. You stir. I feel your titties swell and harden to my palm.

"There—we shall talk. Elizabeth—but talk—I promise you."

"You strapped Phillipa last night. I heard."

"You *heard*? I thought you fast asleep. You did not mind?"

What madness is upon me now that I should so excuse myself, abase my own desires, seek your permissions who wilful sit and cloud my mind with doubts?

"Why did you? Was she naughty, then?"

"She came back late. Is that not cause for it?"

You fiddle fingers one upon another, breathing slow when I would have you agitated at the least and swooning in my arms, drawers down, the deed near done or so about to be. And yet I find myself bemused, intentions put to rout, the old uncertainties returned. Will you not speak? I watch your lips. They do not move. I who should be as master feel as servant now, a footman waiting on command, should lay you down, bring my commander up between your thighs, but know it's not the time for it. Indeed, you seem to read my thoughts. Women often have such intuitions.

"You must not force me to!"

My hand sprung out by force in your sudden movement, you jump up, sit upon a chair, stare for a moment at my prick's hard upward thrust beneath my trousers and then look away.

"I did not force. You came to it." I mumble, yet is pleading in my tone.

"I know I did. Will you strap Phillipa again?"

The question brings a twinkle to my eyes, so pertly is it put, demanding answer.

"I may. May I sit near you? May I not?" Brazen in the poking of my cock, I rise and take seat on the rolled arm of your chair. Your shoulders tighten but you do not budge. "Tompkins is idle—needs the birch at least. Or strap," I do add hastily. My words ameliorate, it seems. A small smile twitches at the corner of your mouth, then like a darting swallow's gone.

"I would not cane again, you know. Poor Agatha— Lord Brearley's daughter—how she cried! Miss Atherton—she held her down across a desk. I gave her six upon instructions, thought it done too hard, but Miss Atherton said not, for Agatha was wilful, would not take to it nor even to her spankings long before she got there. Taller than me she was and such long legs." You are at gabble now, released. I comb my fingers lightly through your hair, make sounds as might encourage you. "Her bottom! Oh, I streaked it so!"

"As I did you?"

"Oh, that was not so hard." You look away, will not address me straight but speak with head turned slightly as though to another. I do not mind, for seemingly am come to this and yet may bend the moment to my will.

"My thumb was in you tight—right up between your bottom cheeks, my love. And was it so with Agatha? Dear love, let us speak clear if only speech we may obtain as yet."

"I should not . . . oh . . . well, yes. Miss Atherton did. Besides, she was a tease, that Agatha, ever wore her stockings black and corsets too, all trimmed with lace, flouted herself about, was over-proud, stepped haughtily, wore boots up to her knees. Lord Brearley came, took her away, then brought her back the morning after. That was strange. So moody was she and then was caned anew. Her howls filled all the corridors, you know."

Old-fashioned is your tone. Have you of a sudden aged beyond my knowing?

"And yours?"

"I did not squeal that much—did not."

"But now?"

"I won't be made to—won't!" Jack-in-the-box you spring, pace all about, then sit upon the bed.

"Let us drink, my pet. Some wine? Come, let us be at ease. How you have changed!"

"I do not think I have. I did obey. Miss Atherton was nice, quite nice, besides."

"Nice?" My voice at squeak. A comedy is here. The wine is poured. I stand before you offering both glass and vision of my upright tool. Your eyes should glaze. In all my fantasies they have. Instead, your limpid stare at it is brief as though it were but a banana on a plate.

"Sometimes she was. I suppose if I resisted you would seize and cane me still." A sidelong glance from you, but quick.

"That cannot be the way."

"I know. Miss Atherton said our bottoms must be willingly put up, though a *little* struggle would not come amiss."

"Shall yours not be again? Your bottom was willingly put up to me last night."

You cross your legs, have self-possession now and swing your toes. "Shall you cane Tompkins—Mabel— then? Why would you so? You said you would or might, I can't remember. The poor dear thing, you'll do it much too hard, I know you will. If must you must, then use the strap."

"I did not cane you hard. You have already said as much."

"Was that not different?" Your eyes in mine that dwell not longer than a pebble thrown by boys skims far across a pond and sinks.

I should not nod to that, should not, and yet I do, as though we savants shared a secret now.

"Or you might strap her, too, Elizabeth."

The daring venture's put—a kite unfolded, flown high in the wind. Avoiding my last question as you have avoided it, I stand a little lost, but have regained a step or two, wineglass at lips, a jauntiness returned. How coolly knowing must your eyes have been in skating the report! Should I change sides with you—or wear a different hat?

"Would you not cane me ever then?"

"I cannot promise as to that—which is to say, no, I'll not use the cane."

"How shall we do it? Will you bring her here?"

"Perhaps. Or when the house is quiet at night. You used the tawse on Agatha? How did she take to that?"

A little shrug. Your face is softened, though. Your eyes do not perch above your nose like birds that wish to fly away.

"She did not make the same cries, at the least. There is a twist to the wrist one learns to lay the leather with . . . oh, I should not speak so!"

"Do go on, my precious pet, my love." I am permitted now to sit again, your hip to mine, a warmth, a blessing from your body flows. Arm round your waist and you do not resist, bend back your head a little to my kiss, your lips peach-fresh and moist. Your nipples poke above your open bodice, still revealed. I feel them gently at the rubbery tips and you flinch not. So glossy is your skin, so swollen there. "As you stroked her, shall you stroke Mabel, too?"

"Poor dear, not quite so hard? Has she done really wrong?"

"Had Agatha?"

You swallow and breathe softly as I kiss your neck and palm your tits more fully than I did before until your nipples stub like thorns, breasts swelling gently, hardening.

"I told you she was taken and brought back, her bottom seared and then was put to bed. In the evening she was made to stand, wrists bound behind her, skirt up and drawers down the while we ate. Miss Atherton then fed her with a spoon. We did not laugh or giggle; it is wrong to do. Miss Majors, her assistant, stood behind caressing her all . . . all up between her cheeks. Thus was she made to do three evenings in a row, then seemed more mollified—at least more quiet. Would she be strapped, Miss Atherton asked of her—although I was not supposed to hear. You see—it *is* done. To ask, I mean."

I have lain you back—surprisingly you do not struggle, clasp my arms and gaze up at me.

"Yes, it is done. Did I not so in great part with you, Elizabeth? Let me suck your nipples, darling, while we speak and feel your thighs. Permit me this. Go on. You were to say?"

"I know not why I was chosen to. . . . ooooh!. . . . b . . . b . . . but Miss Atherton then called me to the study, closed the door, bid Agatha to strip down to her stockings, boots. Was not to speak, though, not to speak. No, please don't open my legs or I will not."

"Go on, then. I will not. But keep them not so tightly closed. How sleek your stocking tops, how tight your garters! You wear no drawers today at least—are good in this."

Your nipples wet, you hot gaze up at me, skirt drawn up where the pale of thighs just shows. With utter taunting you extend them slightly just apart. How slim you are and yet so full your tits and bottom!

"I am obedient in almost all, you see." Flickers of tongue, your upper lip rolled back, but you resist the deeper kisses I would drown you in.

"I beg you do go on. What happened next?"

"Upon the couch she knelt, near-naked as I said, thrust up her bottom at Miss Atherton's command and had her legs apart, held by a rod with straps that encircled both her ankles. Miss Atherton stepped back and nodded to me, showed me how to hold the strap coiled round my palm. I had to give her just the short end of it to spur her on. The splat of it then sounded in the room as I caught her bottom cheeks across. She wriggled, sobbed, but otherwise was still, showed me her flare of pink where the leather passed, but then was still. Miss Atherton then whispered to her ear, but Agatha whimpered, shook her head, so I was bid to carry on. Each time I coursed it full across her bottom words were said I could not hear. Still Agatha said no, cried out her 'No.'"

"Were you not impatient then?"

"A little. No—don't pull my skirt up higher or I shall not tell."

"You taunting minx, go on. You strapped her hard?"

"Some ire in me—I don't know what it was—oh yes! How her hot bottom writhed and cherry-red became! I swept it up, around and everywhere while she sobbed on, begged for release, but then was whispered to again. This time she ventured no reply at which Miss Atherton invited me to spur her harder, and I did, four, five, six times till she fell forward, floundered all about, though much impeded by the wooden rod that kept her legs apart, and cried out of a sudden 'Yes!'"

"What was the nature of her *yes*, my pet?"

"I do not know. Poor Mabel will not be spurred in that same wise."

"What was the nature of her *yes*?"

You weaken, surely—tongue slips out a little more into my mouth, eyes hazy, legs more limp that move another inch apart to the sly urging of my hand.

"Don't know, don't know. Oh, let me up! DOOO-WAH! Oh, no!"—but all too late I have your legs a-flounder and my hand soft cupped beneath your mounding quim, my thumb a-swirling over your clitoris. "St . . . st . . . stop! You promised not! HOOO-HOOOOO! I will not let you, let you not, doh-ooon't"

The lips part succulent, your bottom writhes, I slip my thumb within and hold you so while pecking at your lips and all about your warm flushed face. Sealskin and tight the walls of your lovenest where strays my thumb intruder, but holds still. You fling your head back, hands beat at my chest. That we are come to this is not what I intended. Grave of face I rise, my thumb sucks out, and prick-proud to the window go, my back to you and you left all awry, crab on your back and struggling up.

"You have spoiled it all—have spoiled it—have!" Thus petulant you throw at me soft rice of words that I suspect seek answer in a kinder vein.

"You have no need to linger here. If we are to have secrets from each other, let no more be said, Elizabeth."

"What then of Mabel?" Your voice a mumble as was mine but a short time ago.

I turn, regard the furtive mischief in your eyes, thighs still uncovered, nipples glistening moist, pink-brown eruptions on the snowy mounds.

"What of her? Do you wish to strap her still?"

"I do not mind." You fiddle ribbons, roll the soft material between slim fingers, then ease down your skirt.

"Indeed you do not? I may strap you both."

"No! As to that, I won't. It would be unseemly as before a servant, would it not? There must be rules. Miss Atherton had rules." You look as though I am accused.

"That you have now defied?"

"I haven't quite. Not really—no—I haven't. Well . . . a little . . . really . . . you confuse. My hair is mussed."

Your sweet complaint—meant as diversion, as I understand—makes me now turn and come to you. I strand your hair with fingertips and separate and smooth it while you button up your bodice over straining tits.

"As to the *yes* of Agatha. . . ."

"Oh, you will *on* at that forever—know you will. Poor Mabel—do you think she'll tell?"

"No more than you have, pet, nor Phillipa. After you have strapped her and she's gone, I'll take my own due of your bottom or instead will take your words as to the fate of Agatha. Are we agreed?"

"Yes . . . very well. Not with the cane, though, if I do not speak."

"We shall see, Elizabeth. All things change all. Have

I not given you already a fair reign of wilfulness, refusals, petulance?"

"I have told you all." You pout.

"Not all, my love, but you may choose between a burning bottom and the truth of it."

I do not wait for your reply—cannot—for I have taken pillage of your quim in would-be hot seduction rather than in the discipline to which you should by now be fully brought, sucking upon my stem between your riven cheeks. We are both guilty here, have neither totally at disadvantage.

The door creaks as I open it. Memories of Uncle Bertram—exits and entrances. The tennis court will now be overgrown and net a-droop between its leaning posts, the apples brown and rotting in the grass and all the darling girls aged far beyond such memories as they may have of upraised skirts and heated nether cheeks. All Time should coalesce—would that it might—that one might dip, search for and find and choose to taste again the fallen plums of yesterday.

I skirt the shrubbery that serves to shield the summerhouse from view of any who might loiter in the grounds. To my profound astonishment, Miss Mabel Tompkins stands, hands clasped, beneath a rhododendron.

"I waited, sir, like I was told."

I have cast off my jacket, left it on the bed. She cannot fail to see my trouser-sheathed erection in its pride. Are we undone?

"You waited, yes."

Be careful now. I must not seem put out, astonished, lose my throne.

"Miss Elizabeth, sir, she said I was to wait."

CHAPTER
twelve

Place, time and opportunity are all. Thus, had my Uncle Bertram possessed but a modest residence, having neither grounds nor tennis court, might he have led young ladies up the stairs each time they fumbled cards at whist? Eyes panther-like and close upon him would have put him out of countenance. Cries from the bedroom issuing would have had no charm. Such are the rudiments of bliss that one needs space and air to hide in, walls to shelter, curtains to conceal, and tact to muffle all. And, one might add—as I appear to learn—the mannered, quiet subservience of women such as I thought in some naïveté you had been trained to now.

"Did not know how long I was to wait, sir. I saw you both go in, or thought I did, then stood till one of you came out—pardon me, sir, for saying it like that. Am I wanted here for long, sir? I don't as usual do the summerhouse."

"Your Mistress may remark on your absence? Do you fret at that?"

"No, sir, I don't. She knows not whether I'm upstairs or down or out or in, and Miss Elizabeth said not to worry."

"And quite truly so. You will not tarry long within. When were you last put up, my dear?"

"Put up? I don't know what you mean. When I was put upstairs, you mean?"

"Not here, no, in another house—perhaps your own."

"We don't have no upstairs there, sir."

"But were you birched or strapped or caned or smacked? How was it done?"

That I should possess such a fever of asking I perceive as a weakness in myself while you, the Queen Bee, wait to sting and Mabel falters at a quick tug of my arm towards the door.

"It were only smacked, sir."

"More than that, I'm sure. We take a great interest in such matters here. A girl should be well-trained for all. Is that not true?"

"Dunno, sir. Does she wait within? Miss Elizabeth, I mean."

"Of course. What else. You may enter first, Mabel. I shall follow in a moment. Do not dally, girl, go in—go in!"

Such matters are best left between women at the curtains' rising. One has long known that. They can be devious, subtle, more contriving, more persuasive than men can. Were I to enter now with her, a pause would probably subtend as strikes a sunbeam through a window-pane, throwing a shaft that dazzles and disturbs. Should you falter, I will have you both—or dare I do so one before the other? Such things are done, and frequently, I've heard. Had I been in process of corking Phillipa's strapped cheeks when Agnes knocked, would I have then ploughed in and on and waited on her entrance, all eyes bleared? Would Agnes then have stood forlorn and closed the door upon the scene, or entered, closed it on all three of us?

I will not peep through the window, through the curtain-gap, will walk a moment, pace awhile before I enter with aplomb. I have lost my way a little in this venture

with you. Have I lost my way? I am neither on the stage
nor off, nor know my make-up to be right, nor my attire.
Do you discuss me there within? With Mabel? Are such
things possible? Each moment makes the reason for my
entry more obscure, as if I came upon it in afterthought
or had ceded all the ground to you, came as spectator
only, laggard in intent.

A trio, though? The thought intrigues—opens a lattice
window in my mind. Amusing at the least, but with a
servant most unseemly, breaking ranks and showing gaps
that in a well-kept house were better hid.

It alarms me frequently that ruder men than I show
more directness, ingenuity, in such possibilities as lie
before me now. Fellows of low cunning, I mean by this,
who act upon the instant or make rough plots, refine them
quickly, have no hesitations.

Such a one was Henry Wilkins-Smythe. I knew him
not but through his stepdaughter, Emily, had acquaintance with his manners. She had an air of piety that in
itself was more attractive than the wanton smiles of others
and took this from her elder sister, Miriam, a soi-disant
scholar and recluse, reader of devotional works and noble
verse (her hair done tightly in a bun, round face and
bottom pumpkin-proud) who would defend her prin-
ciples, religion and good works before and after the lewd
acts to which both were with firmness led. I cast no
riddles here, for upon marrying their mother, a widow
endowed with reasonable attractiveness, Henry declared
to her his amorous wish, intent or purpose to pump her
daughters each in turn.

She, Constance, did not bridle as she might have done.
Mindful of the wealth she then enjoyed with him and
which she hoped her darlings to inherit, she sold propriety for comfort, wet his face with tears (made amourous
by the fact that each time he spoke thus his cock was in
her nest), saying as she did that she would have to turn
her mind from such as might occur beyond her sight.

Thus Henry to his purpose wended, taking Miriam as

the elder first. Having been primed by her Mama in the most unctuous and beseeching terms that all might do their duty, as it were, Miriam resolved to receive her Step-Papa in utter silence, in the belief that by doing so he might falter as would the Devil from an upheld Cross. Indeed, she received him in her room while kneeling in apparent prayer and was heard to mutter-moan continually while Henry plugged her bottom with his cork, finding it naked beneath her nightdress and kneeling as he did behind her in a deep chiaroscuro of desire beneath a single lamp upon her table.

As Emily would have it, Miriam first gabbled softly and then all but whinnied. One is not certain of such scripts that may have been rewritten in their minds and parsed by days long past that brushed them close with wings of velvet, flutterings of nightbirds, creaks of shutters, flickerings of lamps.

Being pumped for three nights in succession thus, Miriam first suffered it, then learned to roll her hips and bottom more, though never spoke a word, continued her devotions to all written ones and saw herself as one whose inner Self would never be refused admission to eternity. The wanton—slow-born in her as it was with each surrendering to Henry's tool—was like unto a separate self, in a sense a prey upon her and one that would not survive the ultimate eclipse from Life to Death whence but her purity would shine, emerge, her soul complete in its survival. So said she at the least to Emily who came to understand much of the same, or said she did, when her own bottom cheeks were riven in their turn. Virginities intact, their privacy was not, for Henry took to sodomising one in full view of the other, seemingly that each in turn could view the "agonies of bliss" as Emily called them.

In a sense one might envy him. The pair enhanced his pleasures with their quiet, nun-like demeanours and permitted him submissively all tricks, as thus when Emily

sat astride her sister's back, her mouth a sultry innocence
to his while worked his piston deep in Miriam's engaging
derriere and she, supported by a padded stool, counted
the sperm-beads of the pleasure that he spilled.

Such would be sacrilege with you who neither Emily
nor Miriam are. I hold you dear, would entertain with
you a secrecy that now is breached, for even as I turn,
approach anew, I hear the splatting of the strap and Mabel's muffled howls that sound as the far calling of an
owl.

I shall not intrude. It comes upon me that I may not
now, nor shall I peep in surreptitiousness absurd, twiddle
my hands, stare all about as though in a stranger's grounds
I find myself, waiting upon a summons of some doom. I
shall go away, become a potter or a mendicant, disguise
myself among the trees at night and watch your window-
light. Such thoughts slipped through my boyhood mind.
Once when a maid descending down the stairs had dropped
a pair of Hannah's drawers, I sneaked upon them, picked
them up, tousled the cloth about my nostrils, felt the
warmth—for Hannah had just discarded them. Then—
this being at morning and the house a-bustle—Mama
came upon me and I staring, knowing not what to say or
how to explain my acquisition of such an intimate garment, dropped it, ran, and wished the oak tree in the
garden hollow that I might hide within, dissolve, become
a branch, a leaf, loam-mould. Nothing, however, was
said, although I lived for hours in fear of it.

"NAAAA-HOOO! It hurts, Miss—stings, it does!"

"Be quiet, my girl, and keep it up! Your legs apart
now—further, Mabel!"

By heavens, you have the spirit for it in you, as I hear,
and pace with conscious quiet the outer wall where lie
the seeds of summer in the tufted grass.

"OOOH-WAH! OOOH-WAH! OOOH-WAH!" Sweee-
ish! SWEEEE-ISSSSH!

"NOOOO-HOOOO!"

"You silly thing—that caught your thigh. You squirm too much—just push it out to me. Turn your toes in so that you better stand."

"Oh, don't, Miss, don't! Don't want no more!"

"Remain so, then, and we shall see your mettle. Hard were you spanked? Hard were you spanked before?"

"I was, I was, I was—I told you so. He always took my drawers off, made me lift my skirt up to my waist and hold it there OH-HO! It stings real bad, it does!"

"I have no doubt of it. You must learn, you silly girl, to press your bottom up to meet the strap or cane in its descent. So will you come to appreciate its admonitions before your naughtiness begins." SWOOOOO-ISSSSH! HOOOO-ITTTT! "Your bottom orbed! Did you not hear? Hollow your back! Present yourself!"

"NAH-HAAAAR! What are you doing, Miss? OH-HOOOO!"

"Still, now! I tell you to be still! Come, yield, bulge full upon it, let your hips go lax. A lovely derriere you have, my pet. Don't squeeze so tight or it will not go up."

"Don't w . . . w . . . want it to! GOOO-GOOOO!"

"There, Mabel, there—you can contain it, and much more, you know. A finger in your fur now, just to tease."

"THOOOO-HOOO, Miss! HAAAAR! What are you at? I feel so f . . . f . . . funny, Miss, I do."

"But nicer yet you'll feel, my sweet. There good—there good—now buck your hips a little to my thumb. It eases in so sweetly, does it not? Or shall I sting you if you don't confess?"

"F . . . f . . . feels better, Miss—it does, it do. WHOOO! Oh, my legs are shaky, Miss, they are!"

"First time, my love, is ever difficult, I'm told. I'll keep my thumb still while you work your bottom to it, back and forth. Good girl, good girl, you're coming on, you see. Speak not—just gently breathe and roll your hips. Bend knees a little, if you will. The posture thus is also good once you've received it twixt your cheeks. Lay your cheek down upon the table, turn your face to mine."

"HOOOO, Miss!"

"Nice is it not? Clench not my thumb so tight but let it in its easing work."

Gurgles and splutters, rollings out of breath and other sounds too tiny for entrapment.

"Miss! I'm . . . I'm. . . . OOOOOH!"

"You're coming, Mabel, coming. Spurt again! Not sideways with your bottom too much, though. Just urge it back and forth upon his . . . on my thumb. There, love—there love—oh, sprinkle faster yet. You've drenched my palm, you witch!"

"SOOO-HOOOO!"

Then silence, silence as from bells that toll then suddenly are stilled. Would that the walls were glass, but then I'd stand revealed as tailors' dummies in a window do and bear the look of figures after battles when the ground is cleared of all impediments, accoutrements, harness and guns removed and horses dragged away, their bodies leaden on the evening grass.

A kiss! I hear a kiss. Surely I do.

"Enough, Mabel. You will take to it better now."

"I'll try, Miss. Don't know how to hold myself. I feel so stinging, wriggly, all the time."

"Go to your room. Say naught to anyone, and meditate on what has passed. By this I mean much thinking on the matter, Mabel, for your bottom will be spurred again— you understand?"

"If you must, Miss. I don't know how to take this— feel so strange."

"In time you'll come to it with better understanding. Make not too much of it, nor little either. Practice your posture and forget all else the while you do, save to keep your bottom up and legs apart. You understand?"

"I'll try, Miss—yes, I'll try, I will. Don't like that strap, though. Don't it sting!"

"Of course, my dear, it stings. What else! Shall you be brought to it with flowers and music? I think not. A bottom spurred is a bottom won. Much pleasure you will have thereby. Does it not feel warmer, larger, more replete?"

"It does, I suppose, Miss, yes. Feels plumper than it was and heavier."

"You are more conscious of it, and must be. Tidy your hair and straighten up your dress. Take care in walking henceforth that your bottom rolls a little. Keep your stockings tight. I'll not have slovenliness nor sloth."

"No, Miss, I'll see to it—I will. You won't strap me again today, Miss? Say that you will not!"

"Am I the Mistress here, or you? I may, may not—may bring the strap to you or yet the birch. Be ever conscious, ready to receive. Go now, head high, in measured tread and swing your legs a little as you do."

"Yes, Miss, I'll try. I never thought. . . ."

"You will. Nor shall you be alone in this henceforth. Let me see you walk now to the door. Relax your hips and let them roll, not lewdly but with consciousness of what you there possess in ripe abundance, as indeed you do. A fine bottom you have, Mabel. Let it be your pride."

"Yes, Miss. Thank you, Miss."

Into the sunlight now she comes. I furtive hide. Of course, it is better so. We could not have complicity with such a maid who darkling in the corridors might lurk and spill her whisperings about. As to that, as to that, even so I shall thread her yet. Are you prepared for such? Do you know all my whims or scent them as a gundog does a bird?

Upon my entrance you have put the strap away or are in course of doing so and rise to let your eyes greet mine.

"How well you did, Elizabeth!"

"You think I did? You neither knew nor saw."

"I heard a little of what passed."

"Indeed? May we have wine again? I feel a thirst."

"I, too, my pet, I too." My words ignored as well I sensed they would be. One should not indulge in double-entendres in this game. As if through glass we speak. I would not have it so and yet we stand as pensive as two people still unsure of names, identities, placements of past and future in this moment.

"I would cane you now myself, Elizabeth."

"Really? I have not a mind to it, though later may."

"Is that a promise?"

"No. You did not see? I hope you did not peep."

"Did Agatha receive more than a thumb?"

We are at rapiers again. I have the same indulgence to my needs as others have—must press the moment on, pursue. The promise that you made is fractured but not broken yet.

"Yes. Put your glass down. You will spill your wine, I mine if we're not careful. Yes, she did. Feel up my skirt. I like my bottom stroked."

Your silky orb again comes to my palm, the cleft rubbed gently by my thumb. Head on my shoulder so we stand in full amazement of the hour. With care I draw your skirt right up and bring your quim to urge against my cock which, sheathed, still feels the burring of your curls.

"You haven't told. Oh, witch, you haven't told!"

"I was not there within the room—of course I was not, through a peephole saw. Lord Brearley came while she was being tawsed upon a couch. Miss Richardson, astride her back, held up her bottom to the strap. She wriggled, whinnied, but cried not and knew not that he watched, I do believe."

"And then?"

"Will you be ever at your *then's* and *why's* and *how's*? Mmmmmm . . . push it up a little more and stroke my quim. Do . . . do . . . do . . . doooh . . . do make me come!"

"R . . . r . . . received more than a thumb, you say?"
My prick is out. You will not hold it, though, and nudge
your hand away.

"I too-oooh-ooooh! I told you so. At the twelfth stroke
when her bottom was a-flame he pushed his tr . . . tr . . .
tr. . . . Oh! Oooh! AH! Can't help myself! HOO-AAAR!"

Nor I, but yet I dare not spurt against your silky skin
above the triangle of fur that tickles to my knob, makes
senses swim.

"Come, dearest, come—upon the bed, the couch—
oh, anywhere!"

"Don't mess me, don't! Oh stop! No, take it out!"

Lips slobber sweetly up to mine and then with greedy
gobbling fall away. Thumb out and fingers wet, prick
pulsing stiff, I stand forlorn as now you quit the field and
with such quick recovery as women seize, thrust down
your dress and fall into a chair. Your eyes are of a sudden
bleak. I am as one who in a crowded room has performed
some dreadful indiscretion while all stare and music falters to a stop.

"Please leave me now. I must have time to rest, will
stay awhile here, then have things to do. You understand?"

"Of course my dear, my sweet, my pet, of course."

You sink down, ankles crossed, eyes closed. The Rub-
icon is passed—or not achieved. The play is over, at the
least. The audience prepare to move, treading on weary,
dusty carpets to their doom, from one life to another, or
to the openness of cold night air that waits uncaring to
enclose them.

CHAPTER
thirteen

Changeling will you ever be, fickle and inconstant, turncoat, renegade—or is some necromancy here perhaps? In *Tom Brown*, as I recall—and the passage always caused me to shiver in my youth—it was said by a young necromancer who spoke of apparitions, magic and becomings, that "the same wonder would appear in all the rooms in turn." I understood then why my mother had a fear of screens, and goblins from the wardrobes issuing. Therewith also I sensed the thrill of such dark shakings of the mind, the agitations of the trilling nerves, her bottom bumping on the floor in ecstasies of apprehension.

My palms moisten as I retire. You, still and quiet within, what do you cogitate upon and what have learned? That I would by Miss Atherton be scorned, I have no doubt. "Have you not mastered her yet?" I hear her say, or worse, "Has she not mastered you?" There were you all in league perhaps—prepared to make a mockery of maleness, for it is a constant trick of women to appear at times submissive and at others to turn their hips away from one, avoid the falling kiss, the approaches surreptitious from the male who, nudged by sharp elbows, is told to go away.

Yes, very frequently it is as simple as that, and one retreats, having learned the gaucheness of attempting more. Such formidable behaviour I least feared from you, and yet I seemingly have called it forth. Formidable. . . . The word floats around my head like a loose scarf blown in the wind, or *for-me-dah-bler* as the French pronounce it better, as though there were some small gasp in the sound, some hint of ectoplasm on the lips.

My feet slur on the grass. I shall return, open the door and view you as you sit. But no, that would not do at all. You might ignore all that I had to say, little as that would be, for what have I to say? Shall I say that I have come with cane to you who are a seeming Mistress of the art? Perhaps I should take you away; that might be the trick of it—have at you in a velvet bedroom bloomed by quite a different air where you would, squalling, lose your tricksome ways.

Such do I call them in my petulance, but would not say so to your face. Stay there within the summerhouse by all means. Shall you not feel lonely? Stuff and nonsense, you will soon emerge—clouded by summer leaves will come to me. I was ill-advised to send you to Miss Atherton. I see that now. I should have caught you on my own and earlier this year, in some high-soaring mood of quick excitement. Yes, it were better that I had—not drooled out questions, even flirted with you in a foolish way as I have done, nurturing that eager grin of expectancy that arises surely in all males.

I have known such conditions to emerge. There is a pitch of the mind, most often felt in youth, that is akin to intoxication, contains a general feeling of desire but is more tilted by hysteria of a peculiar sort, a tickling of the nerves. In this respect I well recall a party on Lord Botham's yacht off Worthing just five years ago. I am not usually one of a pack, nor have been since, but found myself to be on this occasion.

All were gathered to celebrate the sixteenth dawn of Sarah Botham. Not unlike yourself she was—slim, dark, with high-placed titties, bottom pert. Five of her friends accompanied her, none touching more than eighteen, bright of eyes, all loosed from the stringencies of their Mamas, though innocent in their intents.

Their escorts, though, were not—fathers, guardians, uncles all, and not a female otherwise aboard. I, the odd one out, though making up a dozen of the men, suspected only jollity—some kissing games perhaps, saw bottoms felt, necks kissed, but no embrace too lingering and all done with a flair of absentminded mood, the maidens flattered, entertained, and coming into life at last, their nostrils to the sea air keen.

"Shall we to Brighton, Papa, and see the Pavilion?" Sarah asked.

"We may, my pet, we may, but let us put ashore at first, dally a while and then return. There is a fine hotel where we may sup and squander hours."

Standing apart but hearing this, I asked of Sarah's uncle, Crickham-Hinks, what of the tide if we delayed?

"Dear fellow, we are coursing here tonight," came his reply as languidly as might be said from one chap to another at his club.

I had heard of such but never known its like before. Such occurs occasionally at country balls during the hunting season when the girls are taught to ride, and fair they look in their accoutrements, hats feathered, all skirts wide and loose, tightlaced their boots and warm their calves beneath as are their bottoms in their cotton, silk or batiste drawers. It is a known ceremony in certain circles.

I speak here of the lusty, rich, and little known who scorn the manners of the town, closer to earth than cobblestones, they say of themselves with pride. *Droite de*

famille, I have heard it called—and this without hypocrisy. I have the tinge of it with you, though you will not
succumb as do such girls who in their ridings to hedged
fields are led and there themselves are saddled in the
grass, their horses tethered, chewing cud, while their hot
bottoms to the cocks are put. Thus they remain officially
vierges, yet have been spermed, have tasted, know the
rich penetration of their nether cheeks and then to fond
Mamas return who, knowing all, say naught—observe
the conventions since they themselves once knew the like
and suffered not for it.

Landwards in several boats we oared at evening to the
waiting beach where cockle-searchers prowl at early morn
over the hard, abrasive sand that stretches on a long low
shelf towards the distant sea, their fingers scoured by
broken shells and grit, forms huddled in a chill, enfolding
mist. Landwards we oared and then took foot along the
promenade to Bright's Hotel where, unknown to the girls,
rooms were prepared—the waiting dormitories of sin.

I had no doubt that Sarah would be fêted first. Not
eagle then, I knew not how, yet knew that it would be if
Sarah's uncle meant his words. Seeing his hand caress
her tight-cheeked bottom where we stood all bibulous
and merry in a bar-room, a punchbowl emptied soon
enough—her father fondly tucking back such long strands
of soft hair that strayed beneath her bonnet's brim—I
knew her quarter-ready for the fray, though she herself
may have thought of little else than to be gaily bussed,
mouth taken quickly in a kiss perhaps.

Mouth taken quickly in a kiss. Do such words form
and fondle in the female mind? I would not flourish
speculations here. The female mind is shrouded as by a
series of half-open doors, each blocking the other in a
serried rank and so at angles placed as to afford but
fractionally a view within, around. Their thoughts are but
half-sensed by males, then gone, and if dared to be spoken of by one are denied as coolly as it might be said that

Monday is Wednesday or the moon is green. Such you are, Elizabeth—well know yourself to be—rejoice in it, I do not doubt. Were I to tell you all that I could relate of that warm night, I have no illusion in the matter that you would shrug, say, "Really? Was it nice? Nice, was it nice? How common such girls are! No, do not tell me more. I have no interest in such lewd affairs. Legs open wide and bottoms up? How crude of you to say such things. If such excites, then you must have a taste for it."

One has a taste or not, though, as occurs. I will say of this occasion that the moments were well-judged, moods aptly played upon since, as I say, girls in excitement are at tilt in their emotions. One will follow all, save here and there may be a darting one who squeals and hides.

"Is it not nice, my pet, to have your bottom fondled so?" Botham asked of Sarah, though I the only other hearer of his words.

"Papa?"

She blushed, but in the pressing all about and other fond cheeks being felt could find no room to move.

Smiled at, she flushed, looked down and sipped her drink. Then of a sudden Botham clapped his hands and we repaired upstairs, the derrieres and haunches of the girls watched lovingly in their ascent.

A private dining room commodious and bright received us. Champers and oysters, ham and chicken— well we feasted—each girl twixt her partners at the table and her thighs felt up. Beneath the tablecloth I descended my hand on to the knee of one, Evelina, bared it a little, felt her twitch and start, and found her guardian's hand well up her other leg.

Merry the laughter of the men, lip-biting were the girls—exchanging wonderment and secrets with their eyes, though all stuck fast for words and spurting giggles into cups and spoons. We had essayed at least their garters all before we rose, each maiden blushing, pushing down her skirt as best she might. I had felt the flesh, silksmooth,

of Evelina, and my prick stood up beneath my trousers
as eagerly as any then, the waiters tipped, dismissed and
lamps turned down. Uncertain to the sofas were they led,
one maid to two males as was destined for them.

"Now to the creaming of their buns!" was heard from
one more bibulous than others, but his hands that would
have publicly betrayed the colour of his niece's drawers
was stayed by Botham's quiet command, "Each girl's
legs up upon the seat—one to remove her knickers while
the other kisses her."

"Oh no! Papa! No, uncle, no!" So rang the cries but
creamed with silly giggles rather than with apprehensions
as but two hours before might well have spoiled the night.
Perhaps it is in concourse that such things are managed
best. Of all, one Esmeralda kicked the most, but being
firmly held was soon denuded from her slim hips down
and showed a quim well-bushed for her young years.

"No! N . . . n . . . no, Papa!" was Sarah's single cry,
her uncle's hands beneath her armpits gripped while
Botham bared her belly, honeypot and thighs.

Pretty indeed I thought her with her corsage quick
undone, tits bulbing pale, brown-nippled into the hazed
light, her mewings sounding as her father spread her legs
across the sofa's breadth and with a questing digit found
her spot. Her breath hissed out, her bottom bumped, hips
twisting in an ague of sensations as did Evelina's in our
four deft hands.

"Your tongue, my pet, the while he corks you first," I
husky-voiced so breathed upon her mouth, she snorting
through fine nostrils as her quim displayed its lovemouth
to her guardian's touch. I at her shoulders held her while
he bent her stockinged legs right back and, kneeling,
grasped her feebly-threshing thighs to taste and tongue
the salty musk of her.

Participant, spectator—both—I was as witness to a
fine quintet of triplings all around at once. "GOOOO!"—
"HAAAAR!"—"OOOOH!"—"No, OH no, not in my b

. . . b . . . bottom—it's too big!" were heard about, each girl turned over, bottom up, her shoulders pressed and held and hips well scooped, prepared for shafting in between her cheeks.

All took as fine a turn for it at last as any might—save you, save you perhaps. Knob-slipping at her aperture, lust-pressing to her silken bottom's orb, Evelina's guardian urged the nut at last into her crinkled aperture, at which she bucked but twixt the two of us was held and moaned and whimpered as it sank slow up until his balls were glimpsed beneath her quim.

Cruel, one might say, and yet were quarter given in the game, none of them would have known the joys of pulsing sperm that left them virgins still.

"It is a form of training, sir. Their bottoms plumper, milkier become from regular injections and remain fit for the sport in bed or stable, field or summerhouse."

Thus Botham to me afterwards and boldly enough before his daughter said—she naked to her stockings, shoes, by then and fair to be pumped by me in turn. How prettily she would not look, but with hunched shoulders, slurring feet, allowed herself to be upended to my prick, hot apple to my belly pressed, but moaned a little at our pleasure's toil, but would not speak and would not speak, the spongy grip of her enhanced by slimings of the sperm within where Botham and her uncle both had creamed her orifice.

So all were done, and to the finest turn, then limp to bedrooms carried, dreamy as novice nuns, long-tongued and wriggling as we pestled them. None looked more innocent upon the beach at morn, the pebbles rolling underneath their feet. But you will not be so, alas. We have crossed that path obliquely in my dreams, have seen the shadows of the seagulls wing across the sea-smoothed sand, have hastened our footsteps—never looking back.

CHAPTER
fourteen

When Phillipa returns I shall not woo her with a single glance—or I shall have you all. Yes, that will be my way of it—might just ignore you, bring you to it last as firmly and yet as gently as sweet Sarah was.

Entering the house, I call for whisky, summon Agnes down.

"She is gone out, sir with Miss Phillipa."

"Of course, of course—I had mislaid the thought."

An irritation in my tone. I knew not of such outing, was not told. The maid is Connie as I now recall—may well be Mabel in disguise. They look peculiarly alike, but this one's bottom has not yet been burned and rolls in her departing. Emily Wilkins-Smythe, or Miriam— where are you now? I shall read, yes, I shall read— disperse my overheated thoughts, seek Milton for a cooling draught, or Keats for images more delicate. One should be constant in one's civilised behaviour, seek apartments of the mind quite separate from desire, regard the static with appraising eyes.

Appraise. Yes, I shall use that word today, shall have it shepherd to the verbs and adjectives that cluster far too much about my image of you.

But now you enter, sudden as you are, sweep upstairs

to your room and then return in mustard-coloured gown that suits you well, as do the ribbons in your hair. Unspeaking, you pick up some crochet-work that Agnes has laid down and bring the small bone needle to its task. Weavening and moving, snipping air, your fingers stir. The move is quite deliberate, I'm sure. I am meant to be ignored—will take no note of it. Long moments pass. I rise and pass your chair, refill my glass.

"You have not much to say." My humour's bright. "Why did you summon Mabel there?"

I do not mean to ask, for it belittles one, and yet have done so haplessly.

"As to that, you let your voice rise far too much last night. I came to speak to you and heard."

"To speak of what? What speak? Of what would you have spoken then?"

"It does not matter."

Of course, you sense my inner irritation. Nothing is more infuriating than a female who shows promise in her unborn words and then will speak them not.

"If it did not matter then you would not have come— in nightgown as you must have been."

"Perhaps. I was in nightgown, yes. You told me once that words were as dried leaves and to watch the feet that trod them, not the leaves themselves."

"How acute you have become in your understandings! You must have seemed a virtual princess—a queen indeed—against the gaucheries of Agatha."

"She was not awkward—merely shy. You have no understanding of such things."

"No doubt, but then I did not entertain myself with such a lewdness as you peeped at. Nor did you finish your recital in the summerhouse. At least do that."

"Why? I have no intention to. You wish me to be rude. I'll not be that."

"Perhaps you made it up, saw naught at all. I cannot imagine for a moment that Miss Atherton. . . ."

"Phillipa will be back within an hour. They have taken

food to some poor cottagers around, beyond the village. That is really kind. Do you not think so? Miss Atherton said that kindness to the poor becomes us all."

"Such things she spoke of and yet sent you back a changeling!"

"That I'm not. I promise I am not. Are you disturbed with me for caning Mabel as I did? You had it in your mind—gave me permission to."

"Is it permissions we are come to then again? I do not permit you to wear drawers and yet I'll wager that you wear them now."

"I do not. But you shall not see. I do not disobey you as you think."

"In that case you will come upstairs with me. Why are you ringing for the servant now?"

"I'd like some tea. Would you not like some tea? Your whisky must taste horrid, after all. I'm sure it does."

"Come, taste some and you'll know the flavour well— smoke and bracken, hints of sweetness and a heady tang. Why spoke you of my being rude? A curious term for you to use since you with Mabel. . . ."

"What? With Mabel, *what*? You were not there nor peeped. You told me so. Oh, Connie, yes, some tea, and biscuits, too."

Shall I say that I listened? Of course, I cannot. How absurd that I should have lurked, not entered in, made play with both of you and had you squalling just as much as she.

"It was given to me by Miss Atherton that you would continue with your disciplines."

"I know. I have not said that I would not. You cannot do it every day. It is not proper nor is right. Oh, thank you, Connie—sugar, yes, as usual, one."

"A splendid bottom she has? Have you not noticed it?" I say it as the maid retreats. Her ears make burning passage through the doorway.

You nibble biscuit, smile at me a smile that has the

vagueness of an errant breeze, examine my desires as does a Custom's officer one's baggage turn—are too remote yet scarce an hour ago were in my arms, your nipples bright, your skirt uplifted to my touch. Confound you. I shall have you yet, shall make you whinny as once Miriam did, her bottom out-thrust to her step-sire's cock. Of course you know this—taunt me with your eyes and glaze them with a secrecy I know not how to fathom, ill explore. I shall light lanterns in your mind, explode night-searching rockets in your thoughts.

"As to charity, are you not minded to it more, Elizabeth?"

I must always speak first. Why must I speak first?

"Do you not know already that I am? You think so little of me that I would scorn the poor? What little can be taken, though, about? Better the girls were all invited here and our old clothes dispensed among them—do you not think so? Pies fill their bellies for a while but do not repair their dresses, drawers, chemises. If, that is to say, they do wear drawers."

"Which, if they were here, they could try on?"

"Why, yes. I suppose convention would not have it so, alas. Do you think it would?"

"If I permitted it, my pet, what other convention would need be? I say, what jolly fun we'd have! What rummagings, what searching could obtain!"

"I thought that, too. You do not mind I did?"

We are at great pretence of riddles here. Eyes snatch and look away. The rummagings and searchings I intend might match your own.

"A capital idea, Elizabeth. Such as you have, all stored up through the years—all three of you, I mean—would suit: chemises, petticoats and drawers, old stockings, garters, shoes, discarded combs and wrinkled ribbons. A fete upon the lawn we'll have—the young seen in their merriment. Or perhaps we might invite but two or three in greater quietness?"

"Quieter? Yes. It would be quieter thus—more easy to attend upon their needs. A party would make too much bustle, would it not?"

A twinkle in your eyes perceived is cherished and, if real, is as a warm hand laid upon my own. The carriage sounds outside, but you remain unstirred. By some fortune or not, the door of the drawing room is open and our voices carry to Phillipa and Agnes who enter now.

"As to drawers, Elizabeth, you will have many pairs to dispense," I quick remark and bring a fluster to the eyes of those who come upon us. I do not glance at either—look away—as though to say in silence that I have parted from the words by posting them across the carpet's stretch, the grey-red sea that floats beneath our feet.

"*As to*, Humphrey—did you say?"

"Will you not have tea, my love? You must be thirsty from your wanderings. Allow me to toll the bell for you. Why—as to what? Ah drawers, yes, drawers. A capital idea has come to us to cast your cast-offs here among the poor—the girls, that is to say, who need them most. A shedding of unnecessaries, shall we say. In summer one wears not too much beneath. Is that not so? Drawers are dispensable, I'm sure. Well, Agnes—are they not?"

"Such girls to come here? Would it be quite seemly?"

"Seemly, my love? How happily they'll come and go, all laden as they'll be! Cook will bake small cakes with currants in. A punchbowl, lemonade, to quench their thirst."

"Even so, my dear, but is it not too much? We could as easily take the clothes to them, dispense them at their very doors."

"Practicalities, Agnes, practicalities—for some will fit and some will not. Better that they might pick and choose. This very afternoon you may array all out and see what piles you have."

"Of course, if you so wish—but we'll not bore you with our fripperies."

"It bores me not to think of kindness so dispensed. What think you, Phillipa?" I ask.

Eyes guarded, Agnes stares at me and looks away.

"Why, yes, why not? I suppose it would be good, yes, nice." Phillipa's voice is blank.

"At three, then, shall we say, just after lunch? I will examine all in concert with you, count chemises, drawers, and garters, too."

I put a crispness in my words. It seems appropriate— departing as I do, a curtain falling on the silence left, then broken by a chattering of tones. Though not the architect, I have at least adorned the plan with words that were my own while you in silence sat, perhaps approved. You have reliance on me now, as I on you—your semaphore received and understood, or my translation's gone astray.

I to my study, combing words, and think of poor girls, sweet girls, passing to and fro, uplifted skirts, bare bottoms on display. As you have, too? I swear you have. The conversation in our minds—the silent one—was scarce of other, as I tell myself. Will you be monitor of all and mistress to my wishes, too?

The time frets at me, yet I now must wait upon your coming—silent as it is—and ask "What said they? What was said?"

"I told them that I wore no drawers. Would of good willingness give all away."

"And they?"

"Oh, Phillipa was *quite* put out. Said I should wear them. Yes—they both said that."

"Then I shall have theirs off this afternoon."

"You will?"

You bite your lip and smile, look down and note my prominence. I draw you to me and you sag, arms loose about my neck.

"Fetch the cane from the summerhouse, Elizabeth."

"What? Eh? And hide it underneath my skirt? You mean it? Really do? There are pretty girls in the village—

three at least. They are not coming yet, though." So you laugh and turn your back on me, but sensuous murmur as I take your hips and feel your bottom to my hard prick pressed.

"Will you not let me put it in, my love, right up between your darling cheeks where I so long to sperm you?"

"Naughty thing! I'm sure that yours is far too big to go up there. You know it is. No—don't pull up my skirt—please don't. Not yet at least. You later may if you are good. You mean to cane them, really do?"

"And when I do will you but stand and watch?"

"Oh, tush, you should not say such things. We'll see. I'll wager that you will not dare! We'll see."

"Elizabeth, my love, my only. . . ."

"Shush!"

You break from me, open the door and mischievous within the doorway stand, one foot within, one foot without, then with a wriggle of your hips are gone.

CHAPTER
fifteen

The stranger women are—the more perverse—the more
one loves them. I have waited long upon a moment such
as this, though little may have realised it until I sought to
bring you to my will. The unexpected arrival of an experience not consciously sought brings with it frequently
a sense of *deja vu*, or perhaps it is that one has thought
of the event before, forgotten it, then come upon it rather
as one might a photograph once glimpsed but briefly. It
is perfectly possible, I believe, to have memories of what
has apparently never been, as if one had lived before,
had shuffled back through Time or even sideways among
its many corridors, much as one strolls through an old,
abandoned house, believing it full known to one—this
wall or that, this inglenook, this flight of stairs, this inlet
by a fireplace, all of which encompass memories that, it
may be, pass from one mind to another. I recall my
mother twice humming a tune that was then at that moment present in my head, and I remarking that to her, she
looked not too surprised.

Massed on the bed in Agnes' room, chemises, drawers, stockings, corsets are rumpled, piled and inter-
twined. She has a certain look upon her face that knows

not whether to be set or melt. Phillipa poses as she might in church, fearing to cough, hands linked before her neat while you stand by the door where I have placed you with discretion as we entered.

"Are all your drawers here, Agnes, Phillipa—are all?"

"Save for our new ones, yes, and those that we have on. As things grow old, of course—well, later, as I mean." A smile attempted falters, dies.

"As things grow old, as things grow old, why yes. But such as you have on will be well-warmed for offering. Yours, too, Phillipa."

"Why, Humphrey dear, you joke of course! Besides, it is not proper so to speak."

"I joke not, Agnes, no. By making one small sacrifice—to take them off, that is—you will have shown how warm your heart is, too. Elizabeth, I understand, wears none and hence has none to add. Is that not so, Elizabeth?"

I turn to you, receive a nod that neither intimate nor distant is.

"Elizabeth *should* wear them, dear. Besides, such words do not become a moment of great charity."

"In bedrooms do they not become so? Here where drawers are always taken off? You make too much of it, my pet. Drawers are impediments—no more. A woman in chemise and stockings, boots or shoes, looks more delightful than when dressed, all humped up as she is with bodice, frills and furbelows, an outer skirt that shows not even shapely calves. Is it not unhealthy so to dress? Do you not think so—do not think?"

"In privacy perhaps." The lips of Agnes purse.

"Good. So we are agreed. We are in private here. The servants may not enter, nor shall strangers come, nor apparitions, peepings through the walls, nor keyholes pierced by eager eyes. Elizabeth stands guardian at the door where I have wished her to. Obedience becomes her well. You first, my love, then Phillipa. Come, pull them down and lay them on the bed that I may know the full warmth of your hearts."

"Humphrey, you would shame us, really! Let us have an end to this. Elizabeth and Phillipa, please come. We'll go downstairs and. . . ."

"No, my love, you'll not. We have, it seems, a surplus of modesty and you, Agnes, the culprit here. A fine example do you set? And Phillipa has spoken not."

"She does not dare to in your presence and on such a subject, Humphrey. I must insist you let us out."

She stares at me. You move. To my astonishment you move, turn the brass handle now and let the door swing wide.

"Thank you Elizabeth. The shameful man! Come, Phillipa, we'll to Aunt Mildred's go."

"No. Phillipa will stay." Your sweet, clipped voice stuns her to silence on the threshold's yawn.

"Will stay?" Agnes' voice has caught a squeak. "She must not, no, nor you, my little darling, come, for he is in the worst of moods—the silliest indeed. We'll take the carriage, have a lovely drive and. . . ."

"Agnes—go!"

I thunder past you, take her arm and lead her hot-faced through into my room—across that small, sad wasteland that I spoke of heretofore—and close the inner door. Her mouth is open, eyes are dull.

"Why do you do this, Humphrey? I don't understand! Why should you want. . . ."

"Well in the night you understood Agnes, and shall again. Take to the garden with your parasol and I shall to you later—at my will. Leave first your drawers, though, on the bed, or you will have the hottest bottom of them all. I am understood, I believe? Am I understood?"

"I beg you, Humphrey, in this fearsome path you take
. . . ."

"Fearsome, you say, yet knew the joy of it last night! Shall I repeat to Phillipa what you then said of her?"

"Why, goodness, no! It was said in haste. I meant no harm nor rudeness, dear, I swear, but over-excited as I then became. . . . Forgive me, sweet. Is that the cause of this?"

"The cause? The cause, Agnes, is just. No wilful bottoms here shall sway nor hips retract when out-thrust they should be, as was the case with Phillipa—and that, if I dare say so, on your bidding, was it not?"

"Yes, Humphrey, but. . . ."

"You knew I would remove her drawers—fumbled and fretted at the thought of it while waiting in your room last night, and grew to excitation as you did. Boldly she offered up her derriere, my pet, as you must, too, who take such tricksome ways as to deny that which has pleasured you. I'll not have these alarms, or would you go within again and have your bottom bared before the girls? Hold up your skirts—let me untie the bows. Brown silk indeed! I much prefer them blue if they are to be worn at all. Now, quickly down and off your feet!"

"H . . . H . . . Humphrey! WHOOOOO! Your finger! Nooo! The girls might venture in! Oh, stop!"

"They will, my pet, if you so carry on. Come, part yor legs more now that they are off and flex your knees, hands on my shoulders in a posture of obedience. You witch— I swear you're coming on!"

"You . . . you . . . you make me! Darling, on the bed—oh, please!"

"Not yet, my pet. Lie down and cool your ardour as you will." My finger at her clitty twirls and brings her on to oil my palm in such abundance that her knees sag more, her breath hush-rushing in my mouth, her tongue broad as a cow's tongue laps about around my own.

"Do me!" Her breathless cry is made—so sweet, I bend to kiss her lips, caress her thighs as on the bed she hapless flops.

"Later we'll joust, my pet, your bottom heated by the whistling cane or hissing strap as soon it must be."

"I d . . . d . . . did not mean to disobey! You'll make us naughty all."

"If it's so called, though I do not believe it so to be. I'll not have arrogance nor wilful deeds, feet petulant and stamping, bottoms covered up, lips pursed nor shakings of the head nor hidden tongues nor whisperings nor stockings wrinkled round the thighs when they should all be drawn up neat and taut."

"Do not uncover Phillipa before Elizabeth! Do send the dear child out, for though I understand her not she saved me from the shame of it."

"The shame? You play the selfsame chords anew! A child no longer, but a woman now. Were you not brought to ecstasy, erotic pleasures in the night, by what you viewed?"

"Yes, well—yes, well—and I confessed it, did I not, but Humphrey. . . ."

"Dear Agnes, had you stayed, obeyed, all would be over now."

A huge sigh from her soft explodes. Her eyes are furtive around my hidden, risen stalk that noses up its crest before her eyes.

"I will then, if you really want me to."

"The moment's not appropriate, my love—is gone. Let me attend to what must be attended to."

She chews upon my words and with a girlishness appropriate to the moment rises to embrace me, skirt looped up that I might feel the languor of her thighs.

"You'll come down later, Humphrey? Soon? Say that you will."

"Are you not my consort, and they handmaidens to us both?"

I kiss her with true fondness, pat her bottom, re-adjust her gown and lead her out. Flowers bloom a little later sometimes than one thinks they may. So it appears with Agnes whose fingers for a moment touch my straining tool and feel it through my trouser cloth. Her eyes appeal and then she turns away, descends reluctantly the winding stair, though not with shoulders bowed. I would not have it so.

CHAPTER
sixteen

I have noticed that in visiting one's doctor or dentist and being caused to wait in an anteroom for periods that are longer than one hopes or conversely are too short so that one is hurried to one's doom after but three or four minutes, then the mind becomes frozen with a fraught intensity and sees nothing but encompassing, trapping walls, entertaining only a vague and apprehensive awareness of the shapes of pictures on the walls or the stolid squatting of furniture that has a dead and foreign look.

This vagueness—this seeing as if through rippled glass—is, I suppose, a means of disowning where one really is, since one does not wish to give reality to such surroundings, nor what they lead to. Or there is an alternative condition in which the mind plays Nanny to one's hunted soul and endeavours to distract it by forcing the eyes upon and towards every detail of the waiting-room's furnishings, unwanted, undesired as they may be, so that one traces with an intensity of completely artificial interest the whorls and scrolls brought forth from wood by artful chisels on the doors and edges of cabinets, notes mentally the age of such (with irritation, even so) and strays all up and down the straight or spiralled legs, surveys the carpet, views with displeasure usually the tone and colour of the walls and that frequent air of utter gloom that hangs about the curtains.

Invariably—and this in particular upon visiting the dentist rather than the doctor who will possibly in any event pronounce one all but dead—I have risen from my awkward chair, hands clasped behind my back (uneasily aware of moisture on my palms) and gazed out through a window in my waiting, and from such a standpoint, drawn to a fine point as the mind is, have perceived how utterly remote the world looks beyond, how static it appears, for one is generally presented with a rooftop scene, the only movement there presented being of smoke that coils from lonely chimneys to the sky. And in such moments it has occurred to me that the sense of waiting— awed and nervous as it is within oneself—is communicated to the outer world, though the latter obtains only the waiting and not the apprehensions and is seen not as reality beyond but as a strange facade thereto as if suddenly all might be made to crumble or roll back as scenery is upon a stage and in so doing reveal what lies behind, that is to say another reality such as one has never seen but which is always potentially emergent, held back by clouds, the buildings, trees, or even the rising voices of the passers-by.

This sense comes upon me now, portends my nervousness of you who wait upon my will, or I on yours. Agnes is shuffled back among the cards of life. The table is cleared—the players wait. That you should both be waiting in my room is a sign of great advancement. I am wary even so. The drawers of Agnes—her surrendered flag— hang from my hand. I cross the hinterland between the rooms and turn the handle to my own, but find it locked.

A mistake, of course. Your feeling is no doubt that Agnes has evaded me—will interfere. I knock—announce myself. How ludicrous! And worse, there comes a giggling to my ears, a shifting sound as if of bodies on the bed. You struggle with her—have no need to—I am here, have bent her to my will and shall again. The cane will be unnecessary, though you may wish to flourish it.

"Elizabeth?"

Already I am rehearsing my entry and my opening words: *"She would, after all, have rejoined us but I thought it better not so. We are well disposed here, just the three of us. Your drawers are off, Phillipa?"* Or I might (and this all thought in less time than it takes to draw a single breath) toss the drawers down and fold my arms, nod to you to proceed. Three strokes across her bottom will suffice (I little doubt you have removed her drawers by now) and then to playfulness. The mood should not be heavy—no. A touch of gaiety, perhaps— a waggling of my prick before the eyes of both of you. At last, at last. I tap again.

"The door is locked, Elizabeth."

My voice has now a peevish tone. I become aware of my breathing and my stance before a barrier that never was before. Selfconsciousness is doomful in such moments, sets one too apart. One should be lost in the foolishness of others—not attract discriminatory glances as if a judge himself were being meted out a sentence that to the prisoner should go. I have always had a horror of such moments, living out small nightmares, inventing entire speeches before imaginary audiences to excuse myself for that which I have never done. One's mind should not precede reality but rather should invent, control, manipulate it, turn it to one's mood as if steadfastly standing between the moment that has just passed and that which is about to be in order that the links of both are held in one's own hands.

Some people, I believe, live entirely in the present, referring to the past—that which has happened only hours or days before—with studied distancing as though they were at one's suggestion turning over unwanted picture cards or opened envelopes which, though they bear their names, they half-disown, treat them as misdirected or simply not belonging in their sphere. Women, I am bound to say, are far better at this than men, and in a moment such as this—poised on a threshold as I am and visualising the departed Agnes as but a comma in a sentence scarce begun (one that has not even yet embarked on its descriptive passages)—I question with an inner trickling of dismay whether I am in the present or the future, whether in fact Time has slipped from me for a moment so that the latitudes and longitudes of one's emotions and upswelling thoughts become tangential to the plotted line and tend to lead the mind astray.

"Elizabeth?"

I listen for the cane—hear not its silken swishing sound, nor cries from Phillipa. In repeating your name I sound as though I am questioning whether it is your name—which is absurd. An irritation rises in me and I knock more loudly.

"She has removed her drawers."

Your voice a hissing through the keyhole comes, as though you were acting out a part.

"Good. Let me in. The catch has caught or else the key is turned."

"But all is well. We are but sorting out our things, will come down later."

A slurring sound. I hear you move from door to bed— or from the door at least.

"Eliz. . . .!"

Now is a moment when the seeking mind pivots all about as if seeking in a maze the correct avenues of advance and retreat. Such a feeling is commonplace enough when one is caught out in a lie. In circumstances such as this it utterly confounds. The clockwork of one's thoughts burrs on, but nothing works.

By good fortune—or so I hope—you have not heard my broken cry which with some irony is broken off as I have bidden yours to be when heating both your bottom cheeks.

"Ah yes, then—very well."

It is the best that I can do, of course. I am prepared to make my tone of voice sound perfectly normal in the face of outrage, for it is none other than this. It was I who bid you fetch the cane. Did you not do so? Is it tucked beneath your dress? I can scarce allow that you forgot or could not with discretion bring it in. That, even so, is not the point to it. Why, dammit, girl, you know the point of it—cannot surely have turned turtle once again?

Ludicrous are the thoughts that crowd my mind in the face of this contretemps. Should I call through the door to say I need a handkerchief, or gloves, and so effect an entry? As well might a prisoner on his way to the scaffold declare that he has forgotten to pay his greengrocer and should turn back.

I myself turn back, but to my study. To appear before Agnes in the garden now would be to confess a failure— and one indeed before all three of you. To have to wait upon you is an outrage I shall not forget. Mark well my anger when you see my face again.

Thirty minutes pass and I indulge myself in thoughts of sweet revenge. If I benefit not from you, I shall from Phillipa precisely because she has not now been caned. The thought upraises me. I shall have her in her bed this night and you shall be ignored. For the nonce I sit and read *Night Thoughts* by Young—its prefacing title being *The Complaint*, which seems appropriate enough. The poet therein urges youth to turn to virtue and from thence enjoy eternity. Rather would I have myself longevities of sin and those with you as pupil, mentor—both.

Upon the opening of my door at last (I sense it to be you), I scan a page before I casually look up, you waiting with a patience that annoys me muchly though I do not show it.

"Do you like my shoes? They're Phillipa's. She said that I might have them now."

"Are you the object of her charity instead of those poor girls?" I rise and gaze at you with look profound. You do not seem to notice it but trail your fingers on the polished edge of my defeated desk where now your naked bottom should be placed.

"I did not cane her. Did you hope I would? There is no need."

"No need?"

"She has surrendered to you—told me so, and yet is willing to the strap."

"Such fancies do you have in conversation! Was *all* told?" I ask sarcastically yet with an inner ripple of dismay. You guess, and only guess; I have no doubt of that.

"No. At least, I think not. She was circumspect. I have the word right, do I not? Miss Atherton. . . ."

"I do not wish to hear of her. That Phillipa is given to such fancies marks me not a scoundrel."

"Have I offended you? I meant not to, nor do I mind that you have tamed her, if you have."

"She had been naughty with another."

"Yes—I know." A giggle bubbling as my arms enfold you now. Hope flutters back and forth like a small ship on the horizon, seen, gone, seen and glimpsed again.

"Why did you lock the door?"

"I told you that—or nearly so. She has no need of it—not in the wise that you or I would have done it. A girl who has received and struggled not needs only to be caned or leathered for her stimulation, if she needs such."

"Received? Received the cock, you mean? Speak plainly, Elizabeth. Are we not agreed to do so?"

"You are agreed that *I* must. Did she wriggle well?"

"Exceedingly, my love, and ground her bottom cheeks hard to my loins as yet you will. Say that you will and put an end to torture. Do you never want to?"

"Sometimes I do. You must permit my whims."

My lip curls. Seeking to raise up your skirt as now I do, you push it down again.

"You prefer, I believe, girls, Elizabeth?"

"Prefer? I do not think that is the word for it. As to Phillipa—if she you mean—at least she is my sister. It is sufficient to know that she has received . . . received your cock. There—I have said it! You have not."

"Yes, dearest, Phillipa received my prick—both in her bottom and her nest. Much pulsing was there of my come in both her orifices. Long and wet her tongue came to my own. Are you not jealous?"

"Should I be? Is not my tongue as sweet—my bottom just as round?"

"Let me but feel them and I'll tell you so. Are you not moist between your thighs at all the thoughts of it? Come— lie upon the couch with me at least and let me feel your bottom, thighs and quim the while we talk, the way we have done in the summerhouse. I shall not cane you if you do."

"You shall not cane me if you don't! But lock the door. We shall not be disturbed?"

A rustling of your dress. You sudden lie before me, pale thighs bared that know not yet the impress of the male's. I would be first in you to cream your bun, as well you know but even so hold back from taking you by force.

"You have no drawers on, dearest. May I not remove my boots and trousers, too?"

"You may—but then I shall not look!"

You turn your body to the wall, I strip down to my shirt with haste and join you on the leather couch, ruffling your dress up at the back until your derriere comes warm to me, my stiff shaft throbbing tight against its cleft.

"Elizabeth, I beg you—let me put it in!"

"You can't, no, can't—but rub it if you want."

"You like the feel of it?"

"I do a bit. You did this to me up against the tree.

Don't speak of caning me, but tell me naughty things, oh do!"

"Turn your head, give me your tongue, you witch."

With eyes half closed, you do. Lap-lap of fervent tongues, your bottom writhes its small, tight polished sphere against my cock.

"Tell me first, Elizabeth: did Miss Atherton tell you that you were to be made naughty on your return?"

"I thought you did not wish to speak of her." A gurgling rush of breath into my mouth.

"It is the one thing I desire to know of her."

"She did—yes, did, but only at the end of each girl's training and none to speak of it outside her study. She said that with the urging of the birch, the tawse, the cane, we would learn to take the cock into our bottoms, pussies, mouths, absorb the wondrous juice and so excite our partners to more wickedness, but always with discretion, never to relate a single word of it to Mamas, Aunts or other kin save for our sisters who might wish to be inducted, too, along the selfsame path of pleasure."

"Agatha was mounted, though, before your eyes?"

"She was so awkward, what else was to do? I told you that I watched in secret, though. Have you not watched? Oh tell me that you have!"

Against your silken globe I rub my tool. Thumbing your darling cheeks apart, I frot the swollen crest against your crinkled orifice, up-down, up-down and feel you wriggle with a wild delight. Passing my hand around between your thighs, I cup your notch and roll my thumb around the perky button of your spot. Head turned your tongue intrudes more wildly in my mouth, eyes rolling up, your cheeks warm-flushed.

"Let me, Elizabeth!"

"T . . . to . . . to . . . tomorrow, if you want, and then I will, but tell me now, what you've seen—oh, tell!"

I speak to you of Sarah now, relate the history entire, while twixt and in between my words you bubble out your questions breathlessly. How old was she? Were her legs nice? She was not strapped nor birched nor caned? Her bottom, was it nice and round? What did she speak, say, whimper, or cry out?

I am almost coming. You in devilment entire have soaked my fingers several times, jerking your hips and rubbing now your orifice more hotly to me. Small early seepings of my sperm have creamed its ring.

"I have no doubt she had been spanked before that, but one cannot tell. In the excitement of the moment it was hard to tell. Certain it was she did not scream, nor did the other girls. All was a daze of pleasure such as you my love would have yourself enjoyed."

"I m . . . m . . . might! All three of you went up her bottom, then—and more? Oh, naughty thing, do tell, do tell!"

"Each girl took five pricks at the least before the dawn broke, that I promise you. Some moaned, some whimpered, some induced to speak said wildest things while they were being corked. I, drawing out my prick at last from deep between sweet Sarah's cheeks, well oiled and creamed as she was then, Lord Botham drew her quiet upon his lap, there whispered to her, coddled her, her naked derriere upon his cock that soon achieved a second rampant state and nudged its swollen nut between her thighs, much as a peeping mushroom might, brushed by the ridging of her stocking tops. By then all wildness reigned within the room. Evelina—whom I had already tupped—sucked on her guardian's cock while taking yet another in her bottomhole. Emboldened, others followed suit. Encouraged to look up and see, Sarah gawped and stared, then hid her face between the flapping sides of her sire's shirt while he a finger to her cunny and her bottom put to make her dance her bottom on his thighs. HAAAAR! 'Lizbeth, I shall come!"

"G . . . g . . . g . . . go on, do! Oh, don't come yet! I want to hear, I want to hear!"

"I knew then all conventions would be breached, for bottoms only are to take the sperm on such occasions. I, seated limp upon a couch at the far end from the now loving pair, heard Botham whisper in her ear, heard Sarah murmur something to his own, though not a word caught. Then he rose and, cradling her, carried her to a table in the corner of the room upon which several cushions lay. "Speak not," he husked to her and laid her down upon her back. Arms limp, hands gripping feebly at the edge, she lay with legs apart, her pussy shown, her face turned sideways to the nearest wall, eyes open, lips apart. Then Botham raised her unresisting legs, held them beneath his arms and brought the knob of his veined tool to nub against her lovelips. Not a sound did she utter then but only faintly stirred her hips at the first touch of him. Inch by inch he slowly urged it in. Her bottom bucked a little, then was still, her glazed eyes upwards turned to his and half-embedded he thus stood. A mewing noise escaped sweet Sarah's lips. Her knuckles whitened at the table's edge and then relaxed. Another inch. A sound no more than "Mmmmmm" or "Nnnnnng!" seeped from their mouths. Eyes turned upon the pair. All motions stopped upon the sofas, though I believe that neither he nor Sarah were aware of it. The tingling of his stiff cock in her nest absorbed them both."

"Goo-hooo! Go on! I want to hear!"

"He drew her bottom closer to the edge and—as she drew her knees up with a hiss—sheathed in her to the root. Her hands clutched up to grip his arms. Hot-panting came their breaths that seemed to swirl and coil around the silent room where many a lewd tableau was displayed. Her lovemouth pouted around the root of him and gripped his pego like a clam. Balls smacking up beneath her bottom cheeks, the while her fingernails dug in his arms, Lord Botham rammed it in and out, his open mouth above her own yet neither moving lips to kiss for all sensations were absorbed between their legs in that first fuck. Never, I swear, was a more fervent coupling seen, her ankles crossed by then around his hips, her bottom gently smacking to his balls and so a wondrous rhythm was obtained. HOOO-AH! Elizabeth! I have it in!"

I have indeed. Excitement had brought you to relax at last. Your sultry rose, tight as it is, has opened to my knob which slips within, your hips clamped firmly by my hands. Gritting my teeth, I engage an inch, then two. You wail and fluster, then are still. O glory of your tightness there, clam-gripped to the hot pear of my stiff tool!

"Dooo-oooh-OOOOH! T . . . t . . . take it out!"

"No, Elizabeth! Hold still!"

"Doh-doh-don't put it up more—it's too big!"

"Be quiet, girl—you are being corked at last. Another second and I'll come, will squirt my come up in your bottomhole—at last anoint you, as you know I must. I'll hold it still if you'll but keep it in."

"P . . . p . . . p . . . promise! Ooooh, it hurts a bit!"

"The first time tingle-stings: only the first. Ask me to sperm you and I'll hold the knob but just within."

"Sp . . . sp . . . sperm me then! Ooooh-er! No more! Don't put it up more—OOOOH!"

Your rim absorbs my crest entire and tightens round the nut of it. Eyes blear. Face twisted still to mine, your tongue hangs loose within my mouth, beneath my own, as though you dare not move a muscle now. I shall come, I shall come, I shall come. O glory be and in your bottom tight!

"S . . . s . . . say he fucked her fully, spermed her quim."

"He f . . . f . . . fucked her, yes, completely, pet, squelch-creaming as he pulsed his come to the last drop within her sucking slit, then laved her mouth with kisses, threshed, was still, and held her belly warm beneath his own."

"HOO-ER! Had I but seen! Oh, do it now! Right up me, up me, up me, do it now! NA-HAAAAAR!"

I cannot help myself, nor you. In one sleek upward

thrust my cock is held within your hot tube's grip, the pulsing *rondeurs* of your bottom silky to my stomach and your eyes showing their whites beneath your half-closed lids as jet on jet I splash within your globe and feel the tightening of your rose deliciously around my root.

"I l . . . l . . . love. . . ."

"I know, I know! Oh come more, come! Oh come, oh come!"

"My darling, fairest, tightest of them all! Hah-hoooo! I'm shooting more!"

"Gooo-hooo! Oh, darling, push it in and out! Give me your cock, your come, you naughty thing!"

"Sooo-oooh-oooh-OOOH! Elizabeth!"

The panting's finished and the squirting's done. Dazed as the mind becomes, all blurs. We pulse together gently then are still, your cunny dribbling cream upon my palm. Fervent your gripping as I slow uncork and turn you over on your back, your eyes wild lilies to my own.

"Dear Miss Atherton!"

You giggle, "Yes!" then bite your lips and feel beneath my balls. "I wanted to the first time that you pulled my knickers down and caned me."

"Did?"

"Of course, She said I must the second or the third time at least."

"But you resisted."

"Yes. I knew it would be better so—but Phillipa did not, the naughty thing."

"I caught her in a moment when she had the least resistance, I confess. The dear girl would have otherwise evaded me. Had you not brought my prick up so. . . ."

"Shush! I have brought it down again this time. It does so always when you've . . . when you've come?"

"A quirk of Nature so it does, but toy with it, my love, and it will rear up soon."

"I'll not! They'll catch us if we do. Linger too long, I mean. Phillipa may be jealous after all, and so will. . . . Oooooh! How sticky you have made my bottom feel!"

And with a whirl of limbs you're up and clambering over me to stand and push your gown down while I stretch and yawn.

"Tonight in your room, my love, you'll be as Sarah was."

"I have no table in my room, so there. Besides, you shall not, no. Did you not say that we would only talk, then dared to put it up me? It felt like a big cork, I'll tell you that—but still, it does throb nicely and your come all bubbled in me beautifully. I can feel it warm within me—nice."

"Your tongue is loosened at the least. Shall I be rationed of your favours, then?"

"I did not say so. Maybe. Depends upon the mood in me."

"Your bottom is more tightly cleft than. . . ."

"Shush! Put your trousers on—how rude you look! Would Sarah visit, do you think? I'd love to see. . . ."

"Five years ago that was my pet! She may be married off by now. Let me but palpitate your bottom more."

"You shall not, no. Sit down and let's converse. I dare not stay long or Phillipa may try the door."

"There is an understanding in such matters, sweet. Agnes knows well enough—your sister, too, but caution has you on its side, I'm sure. So be it. Shall we venture, then, our plan among the village girls?"

"Of course. You must not do it to them quickly though. I learned that from Miss Atherton. Some are rebellious and must learn the sting a dozen times before they can be pumped. Or else we'll make a farce of it. You know that, too."

"Such wisdom! How grown-up you are and yet so young in years!"

"All girls are more advanced than men. I suppose we have to be and yet still know that we must bend to you. It is a paradox that we must hold both ends of, we were told."

"You have no need to say by whom! I paid then for

philosophy as well as bottom-warming? Good. The better
have you proved for it. A girl who struggles even slightly
gets the richest jets of sperm."

"I know." You lean against the wall and smile, absorb
my gazing up your legs, curve of your hips, hard-nippled
tits that still beneath the cloth are hid.

"What do you say then to my thesis now?"

"That we shall clothe them as we said in undergar-
ments finer than they know about their limbs already.
Then, however, we will add a little education, shall we
not? Arithmetic and spelling. . . ."

"Teaching how to write, you mean! Writing and wri-
thing? Yes, we'll have it so. I hoped you so to say, then
one will have excuse for it."

I rise—I cannot help myself—and make to grab at
you. Quick as a bird, you duck, unlock the door, so open
it upon the world.

"And as to Phillipa?" My question put in jerky tone is
meant to make you stay.

"Do as you will. She likes it—that I know. But if you
fail me when I need it, then watch out! Come, join us in
the garden if you will."

"Elizabeth!"

Once more that taunting smile and then are gone.

CHAPTER
seventeen

There are times when, having acted irrationally or foolishly, and being unable to recover the normal set of one's expressions before the seeking eyes of others, one has recourse to further lunacies, as if to say, "I am not myself—am not myself at all. Pardon the clown's costume I have put on."

Not all, however, are as easily taken in—they quickly divine the root of one's unease or guilt and place themselves in quite superior pose, or do not speak at all, which is far worse. Admittedly I have not found myself in such a contretemps since early youth and thus—as I see now—permitted my elder sister, Hannah, to have the upper hand of me. When at nineteen I terminated the foolishness of both trying to draw attention to myself and yet not, it was through the actions of another—a failed poet, it was said, who rather by accident than open invitation came to stay with us for a week. He was a foppish young man, possessed of no money but a certain charm who was passed around the neighbourhood much as a parcel might be which has been casually ordered from a tradesman and then found to be unwanted. He had the curious habit, whenever my mother was out, of leaving notes for her upon her dressing table which were absurd in the extreme, which is to say that he might write (as once I saw in his own hand): "I purchased some oranges today, but the paper broke open and several fell down, so I have gone to my room."

At first my mother did not recognise his handwriting and went all about among the servants asking. The young man, whose name was Eric, said nothing, but my father—taking note of the calligraphy—identified him, though not to his face, whereat my mother was completely perplexed, feared for his sanity and so forth, at which Hannah remarked that it was a form of flirtation and that he knew not otherwise how to express himself. My mother, declaring that she was far too old for such silliness, tore up the note.

"He wants you in his room," my father chuckled, causing dear Mama to blush, for what was done at parties was in a separate compartment of her mind and had, as she saw, no connection with her daily life.

"If that is so, I shall tell him what I think of this," she replied, but waited till the morrow when a further note adorned her dressing table while she was talking to the head gardener. This one, in rather more lunatic fashion, proclaimed, "There are Red Indians in the wood nearby. Should you chance to see a party of them, lay down everything and run."

I being otherwise alone with them in the house, save for the servants, heard Mama in due course go to Eric's room where he always retired after he had written to her in hope she would respond. There are young men, as I have since learned, who take a preference for older women, as one such was he. My mother, not raising her voice, but closing his door behind her, was heard by me to demand what meant he by such foolishness. I heard then his quiet reply, but not the words of it—a muffled sound as though he would excuse himself. More words, then came the sound of sobbing that was his, not hers. I on the landing just above, strained my ears curiously but could make nothing out save what I now describe. I heard however Mama later say, "You naughty boy!" and then a thump was heard. It frightened me and stirred my veins. I longed to see beyond the door, then heard Mama declare in a quiet voice, "You'll go tomorrow, if I do?" He sobbed again. How ludicrous, I thought! Then came a gasp from him and rustling sounds. "Ho-ho!" he cried and then was still. Several minutes passed before Mama came out, face flushed and hands a-brushing at her dress that seemed more creased-up than it had been.

I confessed this all—that is to say the wicked act of my listening—to Hannah who pleased herself by restraining me with one hand at my hair while toying with my trousered cock with the other, so made me jerk and tremble all about.

"Some things are done to naughty boys. Perhaps she put her bottom on his face," Hannah declared.

"She what?" I tried to clasp her neck, to kiss her, but she fended me off and cruelly tugged my hair.

"Her knickered bottom, silly. It is done by lordly ladies to submissive men. They struggle, puff, but are held down by all that plump and fleshy weight. Their cocks come up—sometimes they spout—are made to look quite foolish in this wise. Shall I do it to you?"

"Oh, Hannah, yes!"

"You are not cowed enough, my pet. Tasting my bottom through my drawers is not for you, though there is one who likes it here. Say naught of this to anyone or I shall smack you hard—deny it all!"

I knew she would—had more of a glib tongue than I had then, could look as careful as a nun though I knew well her ways behind locked doors and thought Mama did too, but acted out her parts as well she might to keep the household quiet and orderly, the loose ends tucked behind the curtains, as she often said.

Care now be my companion as I go into the garden,

find all three of you dispersed about in canvas chairs. You—looking up—smile briefly then look down and turn a page. Agnes uneasy stirs, but meets my eyes. Phillipa parts her legs a little and then closes them, reverts to counting swallows in the sky, would know with longing, I suspect, what passed between you and myself.

"We have expanded our philosophy, my pet—will teach the village girls to read and write, add sums and whatnot. Will that not be fun, Agnes?"

"A message, sir, by horseman brought."

A footman—Grimshaw—glides across the grass and hands an envelope to me. The seal I know, is that of Agnes' brother, Luther.

"He waits on a reply?"

"Sir, no. I gave him ale as he were parched, watered his horse, and off he's gone."

All eyes upon me as I break the seal and draw the paper out within.

"Is all well, Humphrey?" Agnes rises, comes to me. As one absorbed I read and do not answer her at first. Words shift and flutter on the page. The loops are swollen with a sanctity that well becomes a poet, cleric—both.

"All is well yet all is bad, my love. A fire—a dreadful fire—but all are saved. They come here on the morrow bringing Pauline back. Thank God that none were harmed, all saved despite a darkling night and flames that roared."

"My heavens, Humphrey, are you sure?"

There follow now the usual screams, the cries, the springings of alarm. From Agnes then to you and then to Phillipa the note is passed, quivers between all fingers like a bird with broken wing that cannot find its nest. I chew my lip and ruminate.

"My poor dear girl! Thank God she was not burned!"

"Not harmed, not harmed—that is the best of it. All their belongings are destroyed, but that counts nothing to their lives, my pet. We can accommodate them—shall and must."

Your eyes meet mine. We are guilty now of what we meant to do in context of this dire calamity, yet have as it were two minds as I perceive in your expression. So one always is when passing from one mansion of experience to another and, on crossing the intervening space— whether driven by winds of misfortune as now or simply displaced by some quirk of circumstance—fears the exact moment of returning through doorways that, however familiar, have a foreign feel.

Phillipa cries. You, too. All three a-wail. "Our clothes, possessions, furniture—all gone! Dear Uncle, what are we to do?"

"Your sojourn here will last, my loves, until your parents find a new abode. Praise be it they are safe. Let us be thankful for a miracle rather than entertain dire thoughts. Come, Agnes, bring them in the house to dry their tears."

"I want to sleep with Phillipa tonight. I feel afraid!"

With that frail cry you run to me. My arms enfold your waist, feel surge of hips.

"You may, of course, you may, Elizabeth. Give prayers for the deliverance of your Mama, Papa and your dear cousin, Pauline."

"Had we been there we might have died!"

"What nonsense so to talk when in this very moment you are here alive, my pet!"

I cuddle-huddle you, cast gaze solicitous on all and herd you in the drawing room, dispensing brandy as seems most appropriate.

There will be an interval now of the kind that I particularly detest, which is to say that all will be mulled over and picked over, ten thousand unnecessary words to be said of what has been and might have been and would have been and could have been, the none of which makes indent on reality nor changes but a brick, a stone, a twig, a leaf. One perceives such conversations as a slowly rolling sea whereon the first waves that arrive sound only lamentations brushing all about the beach of flurried speech to which one is forced to listen while being already aware that midway twixt horizon and the shore are loping in slow motion other waves that have a different sound and splash more merrily as the moods change, as the moods change.

Phillipa cries still. I suspect however that her emotions are compounded of many elements that have found a perverse refuge in the sad intelligence we have received.

"Come, my dear, let me take you to your room."

"I will go with her!" you say, spring up, but by some chance quite wondrous Agnes draws you back.

"She is best on her own, my pet. You may upset each other more the more you speak of it. Be happy that your parents will arrive safe and sound and with dear Pauline, too."

The words might have been mine, but they are Agnes's. I feel a curious guilt that she has uttered them in commonsense, for devils of desire dance in my mind. A weeping woman is voluptuous in aspect if her charms suffice to be enticing. I have always thought so. Escorting Phillipa upstairs I pass my hand beneath her derriere and feel its weight.

"Don't do that now!" she murmurs, yet her head still rests upon my shoulder in ascent. Her warm cheeks wobble gently on my palm.

"Let it so rest, my love. You will feel better so."

The material creases, gathers in my hand as we approach her room along the corridor until I feel the inlet of her cleft where the ripe hemispheres roll in upon her crinkled aperture. Her bottom rolls despite herself. Within her room I turn the key and lay her, hapless, on the bed.

"Not now, not now! What do you do? Oh hateful thing to do it now!"

"Shush! Keep your legs apart, your lips to mine."

"B . . . b . . . b . . . b . . . don't want to!"

"Yes, you do. How fine the swelling of your thighs, how warm and moist your nest, my pet."

"I will not let you! Stop it! Do!"

A fresh cascade of tears that salt our lips. Lax, wobbling is her mouth wherein my tongue delves circling around her own. My hand explores circumference of garters, thigh-flesh, burr of busy curls around her rich, plump mount. Her legs strain, bend, strain down again. A shivered sigh. She melts into our kiss.

"Sh . . . sh . . . sh . . . shouldn't do it now! Oh poor Mama, oh poor Papa!"

"In grief, my love, you look most beautiful. Yet all is safe—you have no cause to grieve. Come, draw your knees up—let me tickle you about your spot that you may find relief."

"A w . . . w . . . wicked thing to do." And yet her breath pants out, her legs skew wide, her further knee up-bent to show her quim where I have slowly gathered up her dress beneath her bottom's moonlike gleam. She sniffs and snuffles, cries, gasps, sobs and moans. Ever in such moments is a woman ready to be pronged. Breath hissing through her nose, she cedes her tongue and has her limp hand drawn about my cock that with some feverish fumbling is exposed, erect and throbbing in her grasp.

"Don't want to—don't," she mumbles still, back-arching as I tease her slit and feel the rolled lips to my fingers part. "It's wicked now to do it, wicked now."

The fever in her eyes gives lie to her choked words. Her bottom, heavy-burdened with desire, writhes on the coverlet, its flesh explored. Gob-gobble comes her mouth and tears between, my prick up-rubbing in her soft, loose grasp. I gather up her dress more till her hips are full exposed, her belly white and sleek, her quim-hairs dark, well-massed and rolling thick.

"Let me put it in."

"Don't want you to! Oooh! Oh!"

My god, how sleek and warm and moist, how tight the walls of her vagina are! Full mounted on her now I have my legs between her own and both her knees in amourous assent drawn up, thighs quivering, balls to her bottom pressed as round about my root her lovelips cling and with a blissful sigh she clasps my neck.

"How tight you are, my love, how tight!"

"Whoo! Oh, don't move it yet—don't move!"

In truth I cannot, am by love transfixed, or rather should I say love-of-my-cock-to-her which tingles, throbs and pulses in her dell. Her belly ripples silky under mine. Her tongue slow laps. I draw my tool out but an inch, then urge it back again. The little movement makes her buttocks writhe and mine to tighten with delight. Pure womanhood is in her now. Her tears flow gently still, are not of grief but of delight that out of such a holocaust of flames that burn imagined in her mind emerges hot desire, impelled relief.

"You w . . . w . . . won't be able to d . . . d . . . do it to me now."

"We'll see."

"You won't." Her voice a husky mumble in my mouth. "Mama, Papa, will be here. Pauline, too."

"There will be ways, my pet, there will be ways. Now work your bottom to my will and let us fuck."

"Mmmm, yes! Oh do it, do me, do! You've d . . . d . . . done it with Elizabeth, I know. Say that you have. I know you have!"

"Not yet, not yet. She is a wilful one—comes not full-bodied to the cock as you."

"Hooo-hooo! W . . . w . . . will you do it to her? Oh, I want to see! Ooooh-HOOOO! Oh bring me on, oh do it, yes!"

We are in full flight now, legs interlocked, arms holding, bottoms jerking, all. Sperm bubbles in my balls. I have the tingling of her deep. Her cunny opens, closes like a clam, her pleasures sprinkling as I ram my rod, the bedsprings tinkling out a merry tune. Under the heat of it, the ice of it, we thresh.

"Go on, go on, go on, oh let me feel it, yes—oh, darling, come in me, oh come!"

All heaven in her voice and then I spurt, gob-glob of sperm gush-rushing up my stem to flood her tight, receiving sheathe, mouths open, tongue-tips touching, eyes that roll beneath their lids as sightless, mindless we explode with equal fervour, stinging-wet with lust, and falling, falling, falling down into that pit of warmth where all expires, where all expires, where all. . . .

"Will they know?"

A querulousness in her voice as I ease out of her my dangling cock that leaves a snail's trail on her fulsome thigh.

"Perhaps. It does not matter. Had we all the summer long. . . ."

"I know. It is all spoiled—and yet I should not say that. Our poor house! I cannot quite believe that it is so. Do you think me naughty? You have made me be. What happened with Elizabeth? She left me, went to you, I know. We cannot have the school now, or the fun."

She cuddles to me warmly, tight, has blossomed of a sudden, needs the dark no longer.

"Would you then, too, have caned the village girls?"

"I might. Elizabeth is strange and yet I know her ways. She wishes to be tamed, yet will not be, asked me how big your cock was, was it nice. I did not tell her—honestly did not."

"She guessed. You have the look of one who needs her bun well creamed." I smile and kiss her, lying full upon the single bed, feel up her thighs, her gently pulsing quim.

"I don't! Do I? I know I roll my hips. Mama has told me of it often—Papa, too. You were the first to put your cock up in my bottom, though. I never thought to like it, but I did."

"Who was the first to plough your cunny then?"

"Shan't tell you. Well . . . I may, one day. I did not do

it with that Captain, though. He played with me and held my legs apart, but even so I did not. Did you think so?"

"I thought of him upon you, yes, longed for your thighs, your bottom, tongue to mine."

"How strange! I did not think you'd do it to me—yet I did—was shocked at first, but then I wanted it. It will be different now. You know it will."

"Such things as come to pass, my love, are not always as we thought they'd be. Your parents may decide to move away to find another house and leave you here."

"Oh! If they do. . . . I don't mind if you do it with Elizabeth. As well, I mean."

What curious naïveté is here! Or is lust primitive in all such minds as find a freedom unexpected in their lives?

"I shall go now or they'll think it strange."

Sperm-frothed, her bush receives my last caress.

"Elizabeth will not, at least. I think she'll guess, will ask me if we did, in bed tonight. But Aunty—oh, she saw you strapping me!"

"And may again perhaps—who knows? Your Papa never warmed you in such fashion?" My smile is cavalier, my stance a businesslike one as I button up my flap.

"He wished to and did often threaten it. Running upstairs at home I several times escaped his warning hand. Mama a-fluster knew not what to say. Sometimes she called him back, sometimes did not. Once I was in my room he did not venture in, though."

"*On verra*, Phillipa. Tomorrow will bring sorrows, joys—much else perhaps. Lie so, your legs apart. You truly look adorable thus."

"You make me lewd." She smiles, lies back exposed, cleft of her bottom urged into the quilt.

"I make you as you wish to be, my pet. Many a proud prick waits to plough your furrow yet."

"The main entrance or the rear? Oh dear—the things you make me say!"

Hand to her mouth she giggles. I depart to make my leisured passage down the stairs.

"You have settled her, Humphrey?"

"Well so, Agnes. She will not wish to stir for quite a while."

"Then she is comforted indeed." Your voice is soft and yet your eyes are thorns that snag against my own and have no softness in them now. Your interjection made, you turn away, chin lifted, too imperious. Agnes regards me with surprise. Is she naive as well, or does she charm herself with ignorance? Or does there fester in her some desire she is afraid to show? I have the oddest feeling in my bones that she would not mind at all were I to spank you now.

CHAPTER
eighteen

Amid the melee of arrival in the late and dusty afternoon, treadings of feet, hands wrung, kisses exchanged,
words put about and sentences colliding with each other
like events foretold, I embrace Pauline and draw her to
my side, would make you jealous with my affections if
I can, yet all my gestures fall into a common pond and
splash unnoticed.

"Have you studied well with your uncle as you meant
to, dear?"

"Yes-no—a little bit of both. Much boredom, I confess, but say not to Mama that I have said so. His poetry
is fine, his tongue is dull. I studied Greek, some Latin
learned, yet ever thought of home, longed to be back.
Have Elizabeth and Phillipa been good?"

"Your cousins, yes, extremely so." I am about to add
that I have spanked them. Would I dare? She, of the same
age as Phillipa, is not an ingénue, yet we have never
spoken of such things, nor has she ever thought of such,
I'd swear, but in the warmth of re-encounter tongues run
fast. I must beware.

Luther approaches and his eyes encroach upon the
bulbing of her breasts in such sly wise as makes me mark

with wonder, curiousity and tingling thrills the emanations of desire.

"Pauline was the bravest. Never did she cry or scream, cloaked all in calm—a wondrous girl." He stands beside us, strokes her hair. Her look is fey, bemused and proud. The women all chat on, chat on. The din of babbling cascades round our ears.

"We should speak of things, Luther. All that is past, is present, is to be. Plans for your new abode must now be made."

I do not wish to say this, do not wish at all. It is foreign to me—an encumbrance, undesired, an otherness. The net of complications that I seek is in the flesh, the darkling nights, coned nipples to my lips, the lazy tongs of fingers round my prick that draw it to the waiting lips of love.

"There is much to brood upon, Humphrey, indeed."

He appears to brood even so upon the breasts of Pauline, the small black mole upon her neck which I have always spoken of as a beauty spot, the sleek flesh not disturbed by impassioned kisses yet.

"We should to my study, Luther, and discuss."

"Indeed yes. Pray excuse me for a moment, though."

The back of Pauline's hand makes contact with my own, as if to nudge, I know not what.

"May we speak, Papa?"

There is a tentative bridging of minds in such moments. Thoughts advance from either side, appear to hesitate, then await an encounter of particular import.

"Not here? You wish to come upstairs?"

She nods. We make our way half-seen, not seen. Luther has disappeared, to coach or closet gone. In such moments one does not speak too soon, but waits, must distance oneself from others first, prepare the fingers to unwrap a secret, since I judge it to be so and feel no trepidation but a curiousity. The stairs absorb us, then the corridor. The brass handle turns, the door is opened, closed. She paces to the window and returns, stands limp, then bites her lip, looks down.

"He may disturb us here, Papa."

"Come to my room, then. He will then wait here upon my coming."

Another little journey made, here to my room where Phillipa doffed her drawers, the high bed waiting and the furniture that broods. Another door to close—another waiting on a moment to unfold.

"He attempted me, Papa."

"Your uncle did? In what wise? Were you frightened, hurt, disturbed?"

"I knew not what to do."

A small, slow pout. My arms enfold her, draw her close.

"Once? More than once? By night or day? You were unclothed?"

Of course, I should not ask this—rather pace about, raise havoc, tear my hair, and yet cannot. Her full thighs tremble to my own, soft belly's curve, refulgent breasts that speak of secrets in the dark.

"You will not tell Mama? Do not!"

"You know me better, surely, sweet. Did you not utter up alarms, cry out? Where was your aunt? Did he possess you full? You say, attempted?"

"I should not speak of it, should not. If someone comes and hears, all will be out. Mama would feel disgraced. I wish her not to be."

"Retire then early tonight. Your room all but adjoins my own. Slip quietly in and stay here till I come. I will not keep you waiting. We then will speak of this before you sleep."

"Yes, very well, Papa."

Suddenly she moves—suddenly indeed as if the issuing of the words from her lips had impelled the movement—goes with that awkward, slouching yet appealing sway of a woman who wishes to be seen, viewed, comprehended, but denies it to herself, is gone, the impress

of her body warm to mine and leaves the air disturbed as
though by its slow wreathing it would fold into itself,
eddies and curls and knows not where to rest.

What would she have me do? Why told me this? The
irony is that I can have nothing to say to Luther of this—
would not dare, am hoisted by the petards of Phillipa and
you, and in the event—were that not so—would still
have nothing to say. What could one say? *"You have
attempted, sir, my daughter but for the nonce—given the
extraordinary circumstances of your arrival here and
taking into account the presence of your wife and daughters—we had best lay the matter on the table, give our
minds to other things"*?

I do not think that that would fit at all. The devil take
it, anyway. It may in her imagination be. Whether Pauline
has been mounted, furrowed, corked, teased, taunted,
brought to heat, I do not know—in truth have never
thought of it. Her carriage, stance and walk, indeed her
figure, limbs entire, roundness of bottom's weight, out-
curve of hips, remind me much of Phillipa's, but I must
not confuse the two. Absurd to do so. Perfectly—yes,
quite. The hours however cannot pass sufficiently fast
before I hear her tale, teasing such details from her as
she would otherwise be loathe to tell, if all is true, if all
is true.

I have no doubt that I should be disturbed. I am, in
fact, warmed through, and also, I confess, amused. It is
an oddity that one can rarely think of one's fellow men—
those slightly corpulent as I am not and entering just past
their middling years—as naked and in the act of copulat-
ing. To say such puts airs upon oneself, but even so
cannot be helped. Let us not pretend we see ourselves as
other than the centre of the world and all our fellows as
spectators, aids, assistants or antagonists.

Luther is at his ease, brooding perhaps on victory, near
gain or dreams of more attempts. I come upon him in the
study, legs stretched out, cigar alight. He has not much
to say, not much at all. His property was well insured.

He means to build again upon the selfsame land, will soon depart. The thought of a new house to him is actually a joy.

"Even so, you will remain for a week, Luther?"

"Of course. We may do a little hunting, coursing—what? Dear Faith is much shook up and needs a rest. Perhaps if the girls could stay here for a while?"

"They must, of course, until your house is built."

I am submerged in small talk—would be rid of it. What he has said he did not wish to say, but wished to say some other, I am sure of it, might well have toed a pond where muddy waters lurk. Some men do have an urge to that, would utter hints of ineluctable bliss, nudge with their elbows and give one a wink. Amusing were it now to see his face if I dared speak of Phillipa's blue drawers, her garters pink, the ravishment of curls around her quim, the tiny lines around her eyes that crease when she's about to come.

Perhaps he knows, perhaps he knows, but I should never think of it, even as he dares not speak of Pauline's nubile curves, her lustrous eyes. I mark well within myself that I have even thought of them who have not thought of such myself before in this same wise. Has he spermed her, was she drunk? I soon must know the truth of this, escape the babblings of the evening as I can and wait upon the night, the night. Will it be mundane or extraordinary? Even as I desire you, Elizabeth, my attention can be all too quickly distracted. If there is fault therein the fault is yours, but ever the sensation of your bottom cheeks still squeezes round my tool. How tight you were! At table my cock rises, stays up stiff. I dare not rise until the brandy's served, the ladies to the drawing room retired.

The time of waiting upon Pauline to ascend is merciless. To be able to free oneself from the order of Time—the perpetual oncoming of the future, instanced as it is in the very progression, letter by letter and syllable by syllable, of these words as I write; to be able to control the backward-rolling of the past which lags in lengthening form behind us as does one's shadow so that one might bundle and parcel it for future use—such would be a majestic and magical achievement. Yet withal there is a paradox here, for at no moment can one say, "This now is the present," since even as the words leave the lips they curl up into the past with as much instantaneousness as water whirls and gushes down a pipe. Thus one must conjecture that "the present" is but a paper screen between the past and the future, or that all Time is continually present and is wrapped in mystery as to its relation to ourselves, for *things* suffer not Time, knowing neither past nor future but only the comings and goings of movements that we perform around them. Truly they decay, though the Earth itself seemingly does not and acts merely as a platform for change. Hence it may be that *things* have discovered the secret of a Present Time which for them is infinitely longer than our own and thus contain their innate stillness in a Mystery that we know not.

I will not do as a philosopher, of course—not do at all. Each proposition that I put to myself merely begs a thousand others for reply. Swirling port in my glass, I hear to my relief sounds of movement from the drawing room. I would rise and enter casually, but a sense of anticipation might betray itself in me. Women are infinitely more sensitive and skilful than men in sensing the smallest nuances of moods.

"I shall retire," I hear Pauline say. A vast relief, though I must follow her with caution.

"And I," you then declare to my dismay. Perhaps to Pauline's, too, for she but murmurs a reply, donates small kisses all around then clicks her heels upon the parquet floor along the hall.

I enter then the drawing room as though I had not heard.

"They will all settle," Agnes remarks with the comfort

of a woman who has known so many settlings in her life, whether settlings of the belly, the mind or the body. Women of her age are much given to being enamoured of comfortable thoughts and come near to tears sometimes when they speak of them.

I pass through half an hour—I know not how—then yawn and look about, but scarce am noticed. I know not why I make a fuss of it. I have but to say that I shall retire, and in fact do. The stairs rise and wind before me like a small mountain of promise. Does she wait demure and sitting on the bed, or fret with curtains—gaze upon the lawn and see the wisps of her childhood in the grass? One knows one's own too well. Better your strangeness and your distancing, Elizabeth, which is a strangeness and a distancing quite other than that of Pauline's. Even so, the proud weight of her bottom haunts my eyes as do the mysteries of her breasts which may have nipples brown or pink.

Along the corridor I pass your room and hear your voice. Not only yours but murmurs that must be Phillipa's—and then the cry of Pauline rising soft.

"Phillipa! Don't hold me! 'Lizbeth, stop it—do! AH! OUCH!"

Good Lord, the devil's in you if I hear a-right and freeze my steps, not knowing how to act or turn or twist.

"YEEE-OUCH! That hurts! Stop it, you beasts, oh do!"

"You sillikins, it doesn't hurt that much. 'Twill send you warm to bed, Pauline."

"NEEE-OW! How dare you! Stop! Oh god, it stings!"

I move before I know I move, or so it always seems when one moves fast, though confessing to myself that it is not entirely for the sake of Pauline but the noise she may arouse. At least I recognise self interest here. Luther has but to catch a breath of all that's passed and all will be in disarray—no petals left upon the flowers at all.

Opening the door I see what I expect to see, but even so reality entrances more than thoughts can do.

Pauline, her skirts drawn up and drawers wreathed down, is held upon the bed by Phillipa. You, as expected, wield the cane that freezes in its motion in the air, and startled though you are still have a sly smile on your face that speaks of mischief.

"Good God, what is to do?"

In the circumstances I can say no other.

"Papa! Oh, dear heavens!"

Released as by a bounding spring, Pauline jumps up, her bottom rich and rosy to my eyes. Plump and pneumatic are the cheeks she covers with a shameful gasp. Phillipa but gapes and stares. The clockwork has run down. All is inert between yourself and she. Gritting her teeth, high-flushed and wriggling, Pauline comes to me, or rather falls upon me as her drawers entrap her ankles tight.

"Papa, they caned me! Horrid things!"

"It was a joke. She knows it was a joke—made no demur when we unloosed her drawers." Thus Phillipa whose calm is quick regained. Her eyes challenge in a way they should not, as she knows.

"You story! Horrid story! I did not!"

"I will deal with you both in the morning. As to this outrage. . . . Come, Pauline."

"Let me p . . . pull my drawers up first, Papa. Oh, turn your back!"

How absurd that something once seen—and full seen as I have viewed her now—must not again be seen! I twist my shoulders, turn my head. You—laughing within you as I have no doubt—look as a cherub might and toss the cane disdainfully upon the bed.

"It was nothing, really nothing—just a game," you say.

"Oh!" This from Pauline, twisting feet, her bottom rolling underneath her skirt. I know her, though, to have been but tickled up. There are no tears upon her cheeks, no glistening in her eyes.

"Some may call it that, Elizabeth, but I do not. You will both attend upon me in the morning. Make not too much of it and nothing will be said. You understand?"

There are nods from both—too solemn and quite false, though no more so than my own awkward speech which springs as glibly as a moneylender's promise from my lips.

Pauline, seemingly, has no more to say. A hiss of breath that may be of contempt, disgust, annoyance, comes from her. Opening the door, I let her pass through and do not look back. From defeat I shall one day to victory with you.

Conscious of silent chuckles raining on my neck like blossoms from a shaken tree, I muse in self-defence that I alone within the house have at least a well-warmed bottom to escort into my room.

CHAPTER
nineteen

"They are all the same! Oh, what a horrid thing to do!"

Agitated she moves, hips swaying, as I close the door, then turns to me.

"They cannot hear us? Cannot hear us? Here?"

"Go to the further side of the bed, my pet, there—furthest from the door. Lie down and rest upon your hip. Yes, so. A cointreau will best soothe you now, or wine would you prefer?"

"Why did they want to cane me—why?"

"There is red or white, whichever you prefer."

"I do not care. The red will do. I thought you would upbraid them more, Papa."

"I thought to, yes, but preferred not to attract your mother up the stairs, or worse, your uncle."

"Oh, he would have liked the sight of it."

Lip curls, head on the pillow, ankles trim. White stockings. Quite adorable if tight—and so they seem to be. I take advantage of her pettish mood to sit beside her, handing her a glass.

"They are all the same? You said they are all the same."

"I prefer not to speak of it. Oh shameless that they took my drawers down!"

"If you do not speak of it, Pauline—if you do not—it may fester all the more within your mind. I do not doubt your word that he attempted you. In what wise? Were you clothed, unclothed, in bed or out?"

She twirls her glass, drinks hastily, casts eyes about, never having to my recollection been within my room before. Her fingers, tapered, long, enfold the slim stem of the glass. She drinks again, knows not which look to wear.

"Will Mama enter? Will she hear?"

"Mama will not, cannot, nor anyone. Wait while I lock the door. You'll have no fear of interruptions, long as you might stay."

"I cannot, though. I must to bed. After such a long journey. After such. That cane stung horribly. How did it *come* here, though?"

"A guest—some wayward guest—who left it here. I had supposed it put away. I know not how they came upon it. Does it quiver you with stinging still?"

"A little, right across . . . a little, yes. He had one, too. A birch as well."

"Your uncle? Was it used . . .? That is to say. . . ." My hand upon her thigh, hip to her knee. Beneath her skirt her stocking tops are ridged, rolled, gartered tight.

"If I did not learn as he wished there were disciplines. At least, he called them that." A sneer, a blush. She looks away, studies the *Stag at Bay* upon the wall. Between her thighs is warmth. Dipping between, her dress provides a pool my fingers slip within with studied absentmindedness. Back of my hand to the smooth skin through the silk. My fingertips to its fellow lightly press. She starts a little, bites her lip, and drinks.

"Go on. I promise not to tell your dear Mama or anyone."

"I cannot say it, though—cannot. Oh, take my glass, please. Really, I should go."

"Not yet. Not while your bottom stings, nor yet while your thoughts dwell within the past. Lie with me, let us whisper. Tell me all."

"I should not, no. Better I had not said at all." A mumble as I stir about, lay glasses down and with a casualness my thudding heart belies come full length next to her upon the bed. She would retract, but then I hold her close, adorn her ear with kisses, soothe with tones.

"You have but to say, have but to say, Pauline. You wish me to upbraid him, kick him out? I will do so on your word, my dear."

"No, you cannot, can you? No, of course you can't. He called me Phillipa! Oh dear!"

"A compliment? Slip of the tongue? Was that so bad? What was the circumstance? He birched your bottom? Surely not! What had your aunt to say of this?"

"That I should be more mindful of their ways and more attentive to my studies. Oh, even as she spoke he upped my nightgown, bared my bottom and. . . ."

"What? In your bed? They both were in your room?"

"You do not understand—oh, no. They had inveigled me to theirs, the lamps turned down and hauled me on the bed. Really, Papa, I did not know, would never have suspected that they. . . . What am I to do?"

"Tell me the truth, my love. Come, kiss, that you may know my warmth of heart. You have no secrets from me? Do you have?"

"No."

I raise her chin as once I raised up yours. Limpid her eyes, uncertain, flustering like moths that once touch flame then veer away. Bulbous and full her breasts against my chest. An inch divides our bellies, thighs—no more. Breathing she breathes, her lips brought under mine, would slip away but then I suck them close, feel for her bottom with my palm and let it lightly rest upon her globe.

"It hurts still? Your poor bottom hurts?"

"A little yes."

"How came you in your nightgown to their room?"

"I was called in. Then uncle locked the door—said that a servant might disturb. Aunt lay with bedclothes to her chin and smiled, patted the bed, said I was not to fret. Then uncle raised my legs upon the bed. I lay beside her wondering. He in his nightshirt stood, then bent, and with one arm around my shoulders kissed my hair. Upon that, aunt threw the bedclothes down upon her side. I saw her naked to her stockings then. Before I could move they had me in the bed with them, between them tight, my nightdress to my waist. I kicked and cried, would not be comforted."

"So you were birched, my love, were birched?"

Hand slipping down, I feel beneath her wondrous globe, the swollen flesh, ripe, silky, bulbing to my hand.

"Do not, Papa, do not! Your hand disturbs."

"Go on, my love, go on, it comforts you. Go on."

"I cannot! Well, oh well, I kicked and cried. Then aunt held tight my arms and uncle rose and brought a birch out from a chest of drawers. I shrieked. My mouth was silenced by her hand and then by force I was brought to lie on top of her whereat she raised her legs up high and wound them round my waist to hold me fast."

"Your bottom bared and uppermost, you then were birched, my sweet?"

"Oh wickedly! Eight strokes I did receive, Papa. All burned and swished across my derriere until I sobbed my tears upon aunt's breasts."

"Her nipples underneath your open mouth—yes, quite. I can imagine the extraordinary scene, the twigs that sought your polished orb, your belly squashed up on her own, even your sex, my pet, that rubbed to hers. Was it not so amid your cries and squeals?"

"Oh, Papa!"

"Was it not? Do I delineate the scene with some exactness?"

In speaking thus I gather up her dress, rippling the folds together inch by inch, uncovering her calves, indipping of her knees that therewith jerk and press to mine. Her hips twist to the ringing of my arm that underneath her body glides. An urging of my free hand 'neath the gathered hem. I have her garters to my touch, the silken bliss of flesh above that swells as bulbous as some orchids do.

"Papa, please do not!"

"Let us come to the moment of truth, my pet. On what long threads you draw your story out!"

"I c . . . c . . . cannot when you touch me so. Oh, pray do not! Oh no, Papa!"

Upon her back I roll her and lie half upon her now, legs bared to stocking tops, firm-curved and wondrous in their subtle, sweeping lines. Her bottom bumps, she stares at me, lies still.

"You are t . . . t . . . tickling, Papa."

"I do not mean to. Let my hand lie quiet."

"B . . . but I do not want. . . ."

"Go on. Continue. What then passed?"

"At . . . at the eighth stroke he cast the birch away and mounted on the bed behind us both, scooped up my hips and p . . . p . . . pushed his. . . . OH! Oh, not between my legs, Papa!"

"It is but a finger comforting, Pauline. How furred you are beneath your drawers, my love! Continue, do. Let's have an end to it. His penis was inserted twixt your poor, seared cheeks, or where?"

Her lips compressed she struggles wildly but cannot break free. Love of delight and warm delight of love as through the cotton of her drawers I trace the moist, warm lips of her plump dell and feel a sweet, betraying moisture there. The delight for the moment is all mine alas, a

pinkness of rebellion in her cheeks. Teeth grit, she twists
her face from side to side.

"You should not do this with me, oh should not!"

"Answer, my love! It is the only way to pierce your
modesty about that cruel event."

"Papa, you are m . . . m . . . making me f . . . feel
funny—OOOOH!"

"It is natural for you so to feel. Your thoughts are hot
upon that night. Fierce was his rod full buried in your
bottom or your quim?"

"Hooo-hooo that you can say such things, Papa! Oh,
do not f . . . f . . . finger me this way!"

"And called you Phillipa, you said?"

A gulp, a bitter mewing cry. I have the cotton in between her lovelips, working fast against the little button
I can feel. Her eyes appear to glaze, mouth opens, I
indulge a long moist kiss of sweetest suffering the while
her hips buck, twist and then subside, and full into my
mouth she sighs, her glutinaceous offering seeping through
where I have made her come at last.

"Why *Phillipa*? Why did he call you that?"

"Dunno, dunno." Her voice is blurred. Lips peachlike
to my lips she neither yields nor does resist. "Said, said,
he said, 'I have it up your bottom, O my love, my Phillipa, at last.' And aunt, she held me all the while and
rocked and rubbed beneath and asked for me to tell her
when he came."

"You did?"

"I moaned, I sobbed. I could not speak. He pummelled
me and ever thrust it up. Aunt worked her fingers in
between us then and rubbed my, rubbed my . . . oooh, I
cannot say! Oh let me up, I pray you, let me up."

"Your drawers are wet, my sweet—come, take them
off."

"Papa! I cannot, dare not, no! What would you have
us do, what would! Let me retire and sleep. I need my
sleep."

My fingers, oiled by the abundant sprinklings from her nest that through the cotton soaked, withdraw. I pat her thighs, sit up, then stand and draw her gently from the bed where first she falters, leans to me, retreats as though to say I am a stranger now.

"Oh, you are all the same. I never knew the like of this! Unlock the door, Papa, please do."

"Excitement or regret—whichever—has in recollection overcome you, pet. Was it then done but once, or more, to you?"

"I cannot speak of it, cannot. All men are beasts, I swear to it."

"Shush, Pauline. Nature sometimes takes its course. Fraught as you were you could not help yourself."

"It was not my fault—oh, not mine! When you put your hand up there and. . . ."

"There—the door's unlocked. Go you to bed. Think not of evil things but dream of love."

"You call it such! I think it horrible!"

"Even so, my love, your knickers did not wet themselves."

My voice has taken on a curter edge. Unfair, perhaps, for there frustration lies. A rage comes over me to tell her what a luscious arse she has. One can take such moods—I knew them several times with Hannah in the past—but must beware of them, showing one's nature at its coarsest, as they do. A finer edge would suit the mood tonight. I draw her to me and attempt a kiss.

"You will sleep well, Pauline, I know."

"I w . . . w . . . won't! Oh, what a horrid thing you did."

"It was but human once I felt beneath your dress."

"Was not. You should not do it. First the awful cane and then k . . ."

"For that you have been recompensed, I'm sure. Hold loose your thighs tonight. Think naught except the pleasure you obtained."

"Oh really, Papa! What a change in you!"

"I will not have you leave until you tell me one thing now."

"What?" Defensively she moves towards the door, but there is trapped within the corner of the frame.

"Did you not think that we might kiss at least in midst of a confession such as yours?"

"Dunno." Head bent. "Besides, what is a kiss?"

"Protruding tongues can make a kiss divine."

"Papa! Oh really! Please! Do let me go! I promise not to tell Mama of this."

"Were you to do so, pet, you would receive a caning quite as harsh as I propose to give your cousins on the morrow, bottoms bared and thrust up to my will. You understand?"

"You have no need to say that. Let me go."

"Goodnight."

"Goodnight."

And she is gone. A swirling of her skirt and she is gone. In the best mood to be mounted is she gone, although she knows it not, belly to belly, buttocks working fast and all her anger spilled upon my prick. I have a fantasy she might be taken so—strapped to a bed, fucked three times, then caressed until her melting mouth at last would yield. A common fantasy, of course. All men possess it at some time—the haunting dream of dominance and love.

My prick throbs, yet this moment is but a comma in our lives. I know it to be so, though know not why. In such a mood the air has a pervasive warmth—appears to balance precisely the temperature of the body so that all sense of innerness and outerness (that which separates us from the world and holds us in a cage of flesh) is lost, and there occurs a sense of oneness, a total identity between that which lies within and that without, so that all things seem possible, already contained indeed, awaiting realisation, and all thoughts seem possible, alert to collapse into reality or not according to one's will or whim. All complexities resolve, all interrelations manifest themselves in readiness much as coats upon their stands wait to enfold, embrace, enclose, may be put on, put off, without demur on their part or one's own.

It is a time of conservation, of preparing attitudes, practising expressions, memorising words one has not spoken yet. They will bring fragments of the past together with the future, crowned with tears and flecked with smiles. I shall be calm and will be seen to be, will wait until the tears have dried and voices have grown calm again, will pick up this discarded smile or that and place it on the lips I wish to kiss.

CHAPTER
twenty

How utterly boring to awake to a new hullabaloo around the house as I feel, on awakening, I am bound to do. I envy those who wake up calm and ready for the day and wonder frequently if any do. All crowds upon one in the first moments of regaining consciousness, as for instance that which must be done (however mundane it may be), that which is incomplete, left over and must be attended on, and that which it is anticipated may have to be done, its nature and duration both unknown. All, all are irritants.

Ghosts attend me in between the sheets, though all will take on bodies when I rise. All save my sister, Hannah, who so curiously I think of yet. Somewhere she rolls a bottom rich and round, one moulded, polished, penetrated, palmed and put to work in more enriching fashion than your own, or Phillipa's, or Pauline's yet. Do Hannah's thoughts burn to the lambent glow of mine, or has she shed her sensualities, become complacent, dull, even perhaps a bore? Of course, I confuse her image with your own, with Phillipa's, with Pauline's, such as all men doing in making up amalgams of their own of merging femininities, memories of thighs, tweaked nipples, finger-brushed thick curls around a quim. All are one and one is all. Only the voices and the habits change. Bells tolled for those long gone—the ones one never knew, forlorn by streams or pendant over hearths, trailing dark skirts along the streets at night, harassed by lights, the distant cries of men—or those who tarried, laboured, copulated, kissed, were fumbled, felt-up, tickled, teased, sometimes brought willing to the cock or not in shoddy bedrooms, stables, sheds or fields. Are gone, long gone, have vanished into dust?

I for one do not believe it so, yet have been thought eccentric, have been labelled an agnostic in my youth, was pitied, prayed for, scorned, admonished, put to task. Once, after gazing into my mother's album and being alone with Hannah (who showed her thighs just to annoy), I remarked on one of a cottage and a family of retainers who stood outside as though guarding and yet not what lay within.

"They are not gone," said I (for all save one were dead), and Hannah laughed.

"Not gone, not gone? Where do you think them then to be?" she mocked, for though like so many she comfortably persuaded herself of a belief—to which I am sure she did not actually hold—of a divine place called Heaven wherein all finally assemble as if in a cross between a pleasure garden and a church, there was also an uncomfortable disbelief in her, a suspension of knowing, as to what might be and what might not when one has died.

"They are here. Somewhere they are here," I replied, for the more I gazed upon old likenesses, the more I became convinced of this, though could not deduce any logic for it nor could marshall my thoughts beyond a hazy view of subtle movements in between the Past and Now. Such time as seems to pass is not always within the past, does not robe itself in "goneness"—or so I feel— but coils invisible, sometimes has not been fully realised

and waits to be again, may then be come upon, perceived
and known much as a song that one has not heard for
years, recalling only fragments of the bars, yet distantly
knowing the shape and harmony of all the notes in their
togetherness.

"They are not beneath my skirts, at least," Hannah then
said, though I knew only annoyance and a sense of utter
aloneness at her frivolous reply. She was seventeen then
and minded to only one thing, apart from clothes, for I
was certain she had already been "taken up"—as then
the saying was (it being murmured openly about within
four walls). I recall now indeed, while I lie in the night-
twisted sheets, of an experience she had not far from
paralleling Pauline's, though without the birch and with
no fierce constraints.

I tell this only as an anecdote, for Hannah hinted of it
to me in after years and had a curious pride in it. In that
year, as I say, in which I tried with total incoherence—
lack of pattern in my thoughts—to philosophise to her
upon the photograph, my Uncle Edwin and his young
wife came to stay. I believe there were occasional pairings
between Mama and Edwin and between Papa and his
sister-in-law, for in large houses such could be discreet,
though signalled by intent and much enjoyed.

This being so—and all done with a passion and delight
that others may find incomprehensible—Hannah was taken
upstairs early one night by Uncle Edwin and his wife.
Upon being asked the purpose of their retiring early, my
uncle replied that they were going to give Hannah a
nightcap. I did not of course know the devious meaning
of this for it was not said lewdly but with joviality. Mama
did not object, nor did Papa, for all three were loved and
nothing made of it. Whether Hannah then knew what a
nightcap was in this respect I do not know. She was soon
to discover that it meant the helmet of my uncle's prick
which was to bury itself up in her fundament and there
delight her while his wife looked on or toyed with both

and then herself was satisfied in a reprise with a sperm-bottomed Hannah witness to the act in turn. Occasionally this was known as breaking-in a maiden and was always done with charm, affection and the little pet made ready for her Papa's cock in turn. Once she had been corked and creamed there was no limit to the sallies she might then enjoy, whether she had been "coursed," or simply brought to bed as Hannah was. A couple were frequently chosen for the initiation, for the lady would tongue the girl (frequently half fainting with pleasure) while the gentleman kissed her and made her hold his cock. Sometimes she would be brought to suck it first, the thick warm bubbling of sperm in her mouth allaying all her fears as to what it might do in her bottom.

I confess to mulling over such thoughts and recollections for far longer than it takes to write which, insofar as another and a new reality is close at hand, is curious indeed. I have no doubt, however, that such an oddity obtains for the very reason that one may tease out all one's strands of thought and shape and convolute them as one may, and for infinitely longer than it takes to mount a girl and satisfy oneself. In thought and thought alone the act may be perpetuated on and on, though there is ever the risk of reaching a high point of fierce, mind-blown desire and frothing sperm into one's conjuring hand at which point all hot thoughts evaporate and are as a crowd of wanton actors, actresses who are caught up by a whirlwind and sucked in to nothingness before one's slowly-blearing eyes.

The simile pleases me more than I thought it might, for here I have my own stage and my actresses three. I shall—I tell myself with some bravado—follow in Papa's footsteps with Hannah and mount Pauline. Since she has been corked, on her avowal, and possibly threaded, too, there can be little harm to it. Her belly once has warmly stirred and shall again. Her cunny sprinkled quite divinely to my touch, whatever her protestations of dismay.

"Women are no more than situations, dear boy," Papa
once said to me when I was approaching my majority.
Mama not being within hearing, he could expand thus,
for she would have castigated him for saying it. He continued by saying that females should hence be treated as
are situations, which is to say (he averred) that in the
roundest terms they are to be avoided or overcome. "One
deals with a woman first, but then may compromise," he
added, perhaps fearing a little that I might repeat his
words and feeling himself therefore required to soften
them a little.

His ideas on the subject as a whole were at times more
primitive than my own. He was given greatly to lust, had
wended my mother into certain ways and she herself had
modified his views—I would say enriched them and given
the rough surfaces a certain patina—by pointing out that
lust itself could be made the prettier by decorating it with
blossoms of desire.

You, Elizabeth, inherit the same mode of thinking, I
believe. The thought comes upon me of a sudden as I
dress. I know not how. Telepathy, perhaps? It is so-called
nowadays at least. How to deal with you is quite a different problem. My promise to cane both you and Phillipa
is scarcely to be upheld. We are too many here and your
Mama will somehow be alert to what you do—though if
Pauline spoke the truth there is an otherness within us all
that breeds and broods by night if not in daylight's hours.
The conviviality that occurs around the breakfast table
after my descent is almost smothering, is like a sheet that
covers the real shape of furniture beneath, leaves humps
and dips, presenting unknown and bemusing forms that
ask to be revealed yet stand so coy.

Pauline's eyes will not meet mine at table, nor will
Phillipa's. Your own dance here and there, are uncon-
cerned. I must separate myself, wait to be joined as does
a raindrop when it courses down a window, merging at
last with others in its path.

Asking forgiveness in a desultory way, begging that I must inspect the fencing around the pastures or some such nonsense—but all said in lowest tones amid a table-babble—I depart, take to the garden and there wait, conscious of waiting and so irritating myself thereby but having no other way to wend or turn against a circumstance that has no reins to hold. Papa, I believe, had all presented to him by the eventual conversion of Mama. He did not have to analyse, twist, turn, invent, compound. His seraglios, such as they were, were located in the house where Mama had eventual control, might send a girl servant to his room with strict instructions to obey (departing all the richer, as they did), or tell Hannah in the most casual way that her Papa would see to her at such and such an hour.

This, I remind myself as I tweak a rose, was frequently immediately after lunch. Mama would see to it that Hannah was well fed and given a glass or two of wine more than she normally would take. A full bladder, it was said, added to a girl's excitement, though I cannot pretend to know whether or not this is true. Papa would wipe his lips carefully with a napkin and would rise, dusting down his coat solicitously as though a fleck or speck here and there counted very much. Once I saw Hannah give a little nod at this, though rather to herself than anyone as if to say, "Yes, I know." She would then get up and leave the dining room whereat Papa would give Mama a kiss and then follow her.

On such occasions in her room, Hannah might first sit herself sedately on her bed and take Papa's proffered prick into her mouth, as she had hinted to me she had done. Having thus excited his corker she would rise, throw up her clothes and present her knickered bottom for unveiling. This being done—and no doubt with an often unsteady hand—he would put himself to her slowly between her nether cheeks which between the ages of seventeen and twenty-one blossomed and grew plumper with all their feedings. Little was said, I believe, there being many quiet exclamations of pleasure on both sides until his reaming piston at last disgorged its manly juices deep within her orifice. Withdrawing at last his steaming tool, and leaving her well-creamed thereby, an affectionate kiss or two might follow before he went to take a well-earned rest. It not—by some peculiar convention—being the practise for the maiden to bathe immediately thereafter, but rather to show that she conserved the generous donation—Hannah would descend as quietly as she had gone up, though with her drawers a trifle sticky at the rear. Mama would smile at her and nod and talk of something other.

I surmise much of this. I confess to that, though having seen Hannah's visage positively glowing and her hips having a certain victorious lilt to them afterwards, it is easy enough to conjecture that all beings are made much the same, do much the same things and have much the same pleasure thereby.

"Did you not know how she would be?"

You have come upon me silently and with the question put before I turn. A blue dress tightly gathered in to your slim waist. The same quiet eyes, pert mouth, small nose, pert bottom I adore.

"Pauline? You speak in riddles. Having attempted the nonsense of caning her—and to what purpose I do not know—you wish in other wise to take revenge? For what?"

"She lies. Did you not know she does? She said Papa was dirty. Pouf! He is the mildest and most remote of men so far as we are concerned. Philippa and I, that is—and Pauline, too."

"I have no idea of what you speak."

"Of course you have. Did you not entertain her in your room last night? Let us walk further or we'll be observed."

With such small words, loose-scattered, I am flattened for a moment. My naúiveté is such that I thought you had stayed quiet, subdued, within your room last night and knew not of our venture to my own. I resort to stiffness.

"I shall speak with my daughter as I wish, Elizabeth. There are matters of importance and grave questions to be raised."

"How stuffy you sound! Do you believe that to be true? Well, I do not."

"I can't believe that Pauline lies. What purpose would she have to that?"

"Oh, DO you not! Then you may ask Papa, and I shall, too. He never lies to me."

You run ahead of me and stand forlorn, a hint of mist within your eyes that has me all a-floundering. In such situations a woman seeks protection, knows that she does and looks to one to give it even though the donor has his doubts of it and feels the ground uncertain 'neath his feet.

"There would be no purpose to it, Elizabeth."

My voice cracks with uncertainty, as well you know it does.

"Really? Then you do not understand women very well. What fun we might have had and now she's spoiled it."

"Come, dear, within the summerhouse. I am prepared to talk of it."

I am prepared, too, for the stirring of my penis to your sultry look. Hands trembling as I wish them not to do, we enter and I take uncertain perch beside you on the bed and cuddle you protectively to me.

"I don't want you to kiss me, Uncle, don't."

"I am prepared to say naught on the matter, if you wish."

Lips parting soft as petals come to mine. I seize the moment, work my tongue within. You struggle petulant, then sigh, relax, and move your mouth reluctantly away. O beauty of dewdrop moisture on your tongue!

"It is not that. She may say it to others and it is not

true. I asked . . . I asked Papa this morning. Oh, how shocked he was! Mama would die if she should know of it. You know she would. How horrid it all is!"

"My pet, then make not much of it, as I shall not. In young women imagination is perfervid sometimes. Well . . . perhaps . . ."

"Exactly, yes."

"You *asked* your father?"

I am slow sometimes to take in all the import of the words my ears receive.

"Of course I did!" How pert and clear your tone! The devil of it is that I am coming to belief of this! "You see now why I caned her, do you not?"

"She had no time to say much to you," I with cunning say.

"Enough. And Phillipa heard, too. You do not know Pauline in haughty moods. She saw me flirt with you and thought to have the better of us all."

"It . . . it is possible perhaps. You speak freely enough to your Papa, it seems."

"Are you jealous that I do?" A little laugh that signals victory. You lie back in my arms and look amused. Mouth parted, you receive my kiss. Together we sink down. My hand, too urgent at its task, gropes up your leg beneath your skirt, fondles your garters, tastes the skin, then parts your thighs and leaves your quim exposed. "I do not wear drawers, you see. I do obey."

"You minx! Were I to know the truth of this!"

"You do. Do you not see, if it were true, I would not dare to speak of it? I knew that she would run and tell you if I caned her. I would then have told you why, in any case, and dear Papa would then have not been shocked. As to Mama. . . ."

"Yes, very well."

"You stopped me, though." A pout. A little wriggle as I touch your lovelips and you sigh, extend your legs, invite my bold caress. How soft the curls bunch all around

your slit! "I only caned her thrice. 'Twas not enough."
Your hand now slyly to my prick tastes its hot upward
thrust through straining cloth.

"Get it out, Elizabeth. Unbutton me. I pray you do!"

"Someone may come. All right—but if I do, you'll let
me cane her for her naughty words?"

"You witch!" I am berserk for you and fumble out my
prick myself, we moving with that awkwardness of people
who would lie together, too much clothed, persuade ourselves full length upon the bed. Uprisen to your waist,
your skirt wreathes tight about your hips, gleaming of
belly, upbrushed hairs all round your quim, your thighs
ecstatic in their plump-silk bliss. "Let me fuck you now
at last, my love!" Rustling my trousers down I gasp. Your
hands strain to my chest. Do not evade me—pray do not!

"You will let me cane her properly? You will?"

"Dear love, now let me get it in. Such richness of
sperm awaits you from my cock."

"You will? Say that you will. You promise, now?"

"You'll let me if I say so?"

"Yes."

"Then very well. But not too hard and. . . . AH! My
god, my knob is in!"

Teeth clench. Eyes wild. I swear mine are, but yours—
your darling eyes—are cool. Your nostrils pinch a little
as my cock at last invades your haven, urges up between
the tight and sealskin walls. Our bellies tighten and relax.
A quivering sigh. Your eyes go soft. Last urgings and I
am within—miraculous the purse of flesh that somehow
holds, contains, receives and quivers pulsing all about
the rodding flesh that you enclose with such possessive-
ness. Silk-burnished are your warm thighs under mine.

"I love you."

"Shush! I know you do. Don't move it yet. How nice
it feels! How big your balls are underneath!"

Tongue lisping now to tongue we kiss. Meltings of
snow and radiance of sun.

"Let me do it now—first slow, then fast."

"No, wait. I want to hold it in. You know I always wanted to. Don't lie so heavy on me, though. Don't crush me . . . ooooh! You're moving it."

"I must, I must! Dear god, how tight you are!"

"HAAAAR! HOOO! It's nice—I knew it would be so! Go not too fast or you will come too soon! W . . . watch me when I cane her—yes?"

"GOOO-AAAAR! Elizabeth!"

"Say yes, say yes—I want you to."

"I can't . . . I mustn't. . . . How can I?"

"You must, you must! Gooo-GOOOO! Go faster yet! Promise you will, oh promise, fuck me, yes!"

"Yeh-hessss!" I'd promise anything beneath the wondrous spell of this. So young your face, so slick your tongue, so peachlike are your lips above, below, root of my penis gripped, vagina working, sucking me within. No virgin are you as I comprehend—and yet the thought excites me more. "I h . . . h . . . hate you!" The words escape and bubble on my lips with love.

"I know, I know. Come, fill me up. You'll cane us all in turn—I'll let you, yes!"

"Elizabeth!"

Down-swirling into lust, yet crowned—as Mama said— with blossoms of desire that softly patter on my heaving loins and dust your belly with their wondrous dreams. Puffing and panting, moaning now, we work into the pink-hazed tunnel of desire. Faint squelching of my cock within your lips that ring me, succulent.

"I w . . . w . . . want to! Sperm me, do!"

"My love, my love, I'm coming! Oh, what bliss!"

Rushings and gushings, lungs tight, eyes ablaze, breath hissing through your nostrils as you spill your creamy tributes all about my cock, balls smacking to your bottom's underswell, legs raised and tight about my hips.

"GOO-GOOOO! Oh Uncle, you are d . . . d . . . doing it! Come more, come more, oh what a hot, thick flow! F

. . . f . . . fill me up, oh do! You'll f . . . f . . . fuck us all like this!"

"All?"

In the drowsy aftermath I ask, cork slipping from your well-oiled quim and drooping upon your darling thigh to spill its last warm-gulping bead of love. Satin your bulb of bottom to my palms as quiet we lie together, face to face.

"We shall not have the village girls—not yet. They'll spoil it if they stay—Mama, Papa, I mean."

"They'll not stay long."

"I s'pose not—no." Your furred bush rubs against my knob. Hairs tickle. All too weak I stir, waiting for resurrection as your velvet cheek comes soft to mine.

"I'll cane Pauline this afternoon—here in the summerhouse, with Phillipa."

"You will?" In part I am amused, in part am feared.

"You said I could. Don't go back on your word."

"Why did she say it if it were not true?"

"To seek attention, sillikins. She may be virgin yet— may have her dreams. It excited her a little, do you think? The thought of it I mean."

"As it does you?"

"Of course. Besides, she needs now to be spurred. Miss Atherton. . . ."

"You never will forget, you minx!"

"Why should I—for you sent me there, knowing how I would be, what I would do. Now Pauline must be taught, as I. That's only fair; you know it is."

"Would your Papa not have fucked her if he could?"

"Perhaps. That's not the point. If she were willing, yes—but not with dear Mama about. I know him well. He has a fear of her. I recall once—you will not tell?— when he and Phillipa went riding through the woods and were long gone. On their return, Mama examined Phillipa's bottom, found it dry, though said not to Papa that she had done so."

Perhaps the naïveté is yours. I will not say so, though, nor shall remark to you of what Pauline averred, that she was called by Phillipa's name the while he rodded her bottom, if he did. I keep an open mind on the affair. It were an odd thing to relate, unless the thought excited her and mayhap made Luther seem more randy than he is, if that he is, if that he is at all.

"You may watch her being caned by me. You said you might. No harm will come of it, but pleasure might. You see, your cock has thickened up! You kissed her? Did you? I wager that you did. No—not again—oh, don't! Don't want to now!"

You swirl your body over mine, legs bump, my stem to your quimhairs is pressed and then you gain the floor and stand, most coyly pushing down your dress. I lie prick-waggling and forlorn, as often you have made me do.

"Come—just once more!"

"Wait till this afternoon, you naughty thing, then we shall see. At three o'clock or thereabouts—right after lunch. Don't follow me. Wait till I've gone."

"Elizabeth, come back!"

"Shan't—won't!" A giggle and you reach the door, blow me a kiss and then depart.

I groan, part pleasure, part despair, swing legs to floor and feel all crumpled up as one does with one's trousers down. Obscene, absurd—well almost—quite—then jerk my head up as you, passing, tap upon the window, smile. And hold three fingers up to me. . . .

CHAPTER
twenty-one

It is said, I believe, that among the Arab race adultery may not be proved unless it has been witnessed and attested to. One does not know, of course, how Arabs live. They may have no doors to their rooms, in which case it may be they copulate in sight of all—the which I doubt for they are also said to be a proud and fiery race. Are we not, too, in our bluff way?

I contemplate Luther on my return within the house. He may be guilty, may be not. There is as much a look of arrogance to Pauline's bottom as a woman ever has. I have no doubt she struggled, is the type that would until the knob is well within the ring and then more easily invades, slips up, is gripped and scarce can be rejected at full thrust. Once the female bottom bulbs into one's belly all is well, secured and comforting. I doubt the role of her aunt in all, however—there's the flaw. The story's too elaborate, the actors wrong. I mind many such things that have happened in other houses, other times, but there's a different flavour to it then—I cannot name it otherwise. The case of young Sarah Botham was a point, took place within an orchestrated pattern of events—a warmth, a cosiness, a blending of the deeds. I see her legs apart, the cock put in, and not a whimper from her. Lax she lay, knees loosely hung, her bottom to the edge of table drawn. A fine spurting she had of it, eyes glazed, clinging beneath, bare polished orb upon the polished top.

There have been others such, in wrestlings, tumblings, hot bouts of desire. One such was Sylvia Featherstone-Lamont who by all sorts of strategems, feignings of illness, vapours, rigid pride, evaded coursings, birchings—came a virgin bride both front and rear when she was twenty-one. Even however as the sparrows wait for bread upon their cold and lonely branches in the winter months when hoarfrost tweaks the nose and frosts the lips, so the males waited with the patience due to one whose haunches were magnificent, though cold as marble till her wedding day.

At the reception in the great hall of her abode that often seemed as cold as she, a great fire roared on that day as it would in she, although dear Sylvia knew it not. Her bridegroom, foppish (and intended to be ruled by her) was drawn aside, assailed by warning lips that Sylvia would withhold her favours from him that same night unless she were ripened to it first. Several of the ladies, not being enamoured of Sylvia's frigid ways and jealous no doubt of her undoubted charms—agreed. Being much in his cups and blurred with drink, drawn into an ante room, his cock touched up by female hands the better to excite his brain—persuaded that a well-spermed quim and bottom would come more obedient to him at the last, or he would live a life of cold propriety—he hazily agreed, hiccoughed, sank back upon a chaise lounge and then slept while his persuaders tiptoed out and gave a silent signal for the joust.

Would that I could describe it far better than I did the corkings of Sarah and her friends. I have a devotion to my task, you see. One day, Elizabeth, your eyes will fall upon these words and fret, I know, at my shortcomings, the failures of my would-be elaborations, trailings of adjectives too poor. I should to dictionaries but have no time for it, chew at my pen and window-stare in hope of flutterings of words more sensuous to settle underneath my nib, blend with the ink and course across the page.

Let the words dance. I pray for them to come. The dear girl, quite caught by surprise in the high flush of fawnings all about, was drawn to a table where a silver punchbowl stood. Without a ladle, I might say. Being told with much false merriness that custom had it she must bend forward, drink a little with her lips and wish a wish, she was persuaded to—had far to reach and so was aided with a hand beneath her chin.

Two ladies then their arms ringed round her waist— one just below and one above. Laughing, she tried to spurn their hold, was told to drink or she would spoil it all. At the first spluttering of her lips upon the heady liquid then her bridal skirts were nimbly raised. "GOOOO-GLARRRR!" she bubbled madly in the bowl, but by then all was lost—or all was gained. So firmly held was she, her hips could move an inch this way or that—no more. "BLUB-BLUB!" she spluttered, had her drawers ripped down and then her globe magnificent displayed, the fur-row gingery, the skin snow-white, her cunny plump but tightly pursed beneath. Pink garters, yes, and stockings cream, thighs plump and calves superbly curved, so much that several women fingered her the while the men their rigid cocks got out.

Beneath the table then her brother slid—one she had spurned, whose lips she would not taste nor feel his cock. Facing beneath her rear and having thus a perfect bird's-eye view (I fear this rude), he thrust her ankles wide apart and held them thus, as might young Samson marble columns move.

The bowl was then removed amid her cries—a pillow

laid beneath her face. One lady who had ringed her waist now faced towards the room and held the prey's plump nether cheeks apart. the better to display her virgin hole.

"No! Never, never! Oh my god!" Such cries as came from her were loud, rang through the then hushed room . . . and were ignored. Her blush ran to her shoulders, it was said. The gritting of her teeth was heard.

I confess that it comes to this occasionally, though not being considered in a closed society a rape but an induction it proceeds as sternly as a birching often does, or blandly is the word perhaps, for pleasure comes upon the victim soon enough. All know it will and hold no wrong to it, much as Mama would say "It does you good" when feeding me hot soup to aid a cold.

"JEEEE-EEEEK!" Her shrill cry sounded thus when the first knob was put to her, it being held there for a moment to her hole that she might know the warmth and roundness of the manly prong. "My god, dear heaven, stop him, do! I shall die, shall die of this, I will!"

No answer came of course. Ringed arms then held her tighter as she bucked her swollen, fleshy globe, and all in vain. Cupping her hemispheres he urged it in to screaming rage from Sylvia who felt her wrinkled rim yield to the first lewd probe, began to sob and twist her head, prayed for deliverance—and went unheard.

"Slowly!" was hissed to her invader while the clawing fingers held her cheeks still, wide apart.

He grunted, nodded and—blind-eyed no doubt—pushed up an inch of it in her warm tube the while she howled, cursed, raved and beat her fists in vain upon the table top, seeking deliverance, though none would come.

"How tight she is!"

The others clapped, which added to her rage, I'm sure. Her head jerked up, mouth open as he gained another inch of territory then rammed his throbbing tool within her deep.

"NAH-HOOOO! He's splitting me! Have mercy, please! Oh Carole, Julia, make him take it out!"

All were impassive at the first. Such ceremonials as they are often called invite solemnity, not mirth. There is something majestic in the pistoning of a full-bodied female as dear Sylvia was.

"WOH-WOH! OH, NO!" Her sobs were piteous. His shirt tucked up, his belly took her bottom's flagrant bulbing to his flesh and there communicated by some alchemy the intimations of desire that soon would come upon her. Soon? It was said that having doused her warmly with his sperm, she sobbed on still when a second quivering cock nosed in and found her better lubricated.

"I wager on the third she'll move and stir her bottom!" came a cry. Uplifted skirts were then and quims displayed, ringed fingers toying with the waiting cocks.

"The fourth! She'll hold out to the fourth! A hundred guineas on it!" was the reply, but both who shouted so were scolded for it and stood quiet, swallowed and knew their raucous sins.

"I hate you, beasts! I hate you all! Blub-blub! Oh no! OOOH! take it out!"

Still naught was said—the interruptions, raucous as they had been, were soon forgot. Breath hissing, clawing at the table top, Sylvia received a second pulsing from the male who had replaced the first, then weak-kneed quivered, slumped and drew it out, sperm dribbling down on to her trembling thighs.

The third was at her quicker then. One saw the easier entrance of his knob, her flutterings of moans, her shoulders hunched.

"HOOO-HOOO! It's horrible!" she sobbed, but some remarked with knowing nods the slight change in her voice as once more she was stoutly corked until his balls were couched beneath her quim. "Ma-ma! Ma-ma!" came Sylvia's weaker cries. Her plump cheeks tightened to the rod, though in and out it moved with ease, his belly smacking loudly to her globe.

"The fourth—'twill be the fourth" was whispered then, for Sylvia's face, full-flushed, had ceased to move. Soft whimpers issued from her lips, her eyes half closed, her lashes tremulous upon her cheeks. Her fingers clenched, were motionless, no longer clawed but curled within her palm. Four dozen thrusts or thereabouts and then her third expended his warm gruel with panting pleasure and ecstatic face, withdrawing slowly with a gentle "plop!" which caused sweet Sylvia to wriggle then and utter up a plaintive gasp. "WHOOO-HOOO!" she moaned, then wriggled and lay still.

"Rupert is next," a gruff voice said. There was no need for silence then by some accord—as if to say she had received and would with willingness take more.

"NEEE-OH! Not him!" her squeal came as her brother scrambled up from underneath the table and with his face quite pale in his excitement put his cock to her in turn. "NO-HO-HO-HO!" sobbed she, but all was lost, and so in that moment of incestuous bliss was Sylvia. Quite against her will, I'm sure, her hips at last began to stir as in and out her brother's penis pumped. Breath snorted from her nostrils and her face, 'twas said, grew puffy with desire since, deep within, her tinglings were exciting now.

At that, the ladies slowly loosed their grip on her and with some watching caution stepped away to leave her free to take the yearning cork. Hands clapped against her hips then Rupert worked, smacking his belly hard against her orb and even drew her back a little from the table's edge to hold her well displayed.

"Good girl, good girl," was boldly said by all, for though she whimpered, moaned and tossed, her bottom slowly worked to him. Legs parted and her toes turned in, she raised her shoulders, straightened up her arms, began to pant as does a bitch in heat, stared at the wall ahead, was blind to all save the hot pleasure of her brother's cock which reamed her foaming hole so easily, while SMACK! SMACK! SMACK! her bottom bounced to him, causing his balls to swing up to her quim at every inward thrust and kiss the lovelips that long had spurned his touch.

The melee proper then began. Cushions were laid, the ladies were undressed, wives were exchanged and even nieces poked. Put down among them afterwards, knees bent and dewy quim exposed, Sylvia received her mountings one by one until she languished in thick pools of sperm, her bridegroom snoring on and snoring on. . . .

Of course, I have not told it well at all. Who can describe the moisture of a peach so as to taste it on the tongue, who venture to alert the palms to feel of satin flesh, texture of curls around the quim that tickle to the surface of one's skin? The gambit's lost the moment that the pen is dipped within the ink, the mind a wild and whirling net that seeks in vain to catch the feel of it.

Luther is sombre and his mind apart from mine. I worry he might raise the matter now, fluster the house with accusations, cries. He broods by a window, smokes, stares into space. It may be that whatever I say now might seem to excuse myself. Frequently enough one shares the guilt that in part belongs to others, as if one is bedevilled by its presence, wants to clear the air, say in effect "There's nothing here at all!"

In the event I have no need to worry on that score. His mind is all upon his property.

"It were best that I return,, Humphrey. The longer that I linger here . . ."

"Why, yes!"

My exclamation comes too soon, is bitten back.

"You'll worry otherwise," I say and give him quite a boyish smile that others more astute than he would read as guilt or a desire to have him quit before he should.

"Good fellow that you are, Humphrey, we'll leave the

girls here and return within a week or two. The preparations made to build the house anew may then proceed."

"After lunch, Luther. You must have lunch." So Agnes interjects and beams at all.

After lunch—after lunch—Papa would rise and dust the flecks and specks from off his coat. Hannah would work her lips a little, rise in turn and, with a fond nod from Mama, proceed upstairs. I cannot relive such moments, though I would. They are behind the walls in our old house—linger between the paper and the plaster, wait to be relived, brought forth, revived, and warmth of sounds, scents, clink of plates, rustlings of table cloths and silence of empty glasses, brought to life again, or rather rediscovered in their realm of what is past yet waits to be once more, much as an empty, silent flight of stairs invites the feet to slowly mount each tread when what is known beyond the silence are the sounds unheard, almost unheard yet faintly twittering like birds that hide among the leaves, dart out and then are gone again.

"Lunch will intrude. We had best make it four. I will have tea with Phillipa and Pauline in the summerhouse. Aunt will not mind, I'm sure. She'll think us nicely tucked away."

You whisper to me thus along the hall, the trunks again got out, the house a-stir. Pauline looks bland, expressionless, and silent moves, disdaining both our glances as she does.

I should put an end to this, should say, "It must be you and I alone," but cannot bring myself to do. The arrangement is absurd, mechanical, yet I am brought to it who knows a pattern set—a maze made ready and the exit known yet half-forgot. I do not answer, but you know my ways. In confidence you move towards the open door and leave me—yes—obedient.

CHAPTER
twenty-two

Im must be devious, I know I must.

"Shall you go out this afternoon, my love?" Thus Agnes asks and makes me all alert. The coach departing leaves a trail of dust. Dust on the sills. The sunlight will not move it now.

"I may. I think I will—yes, will." Therewith the key's provided and I take it up. I shall remove myself from your temptations—take my horse and ride afar, linger along the lanes until the soft dusk folds its wings of silence on us all. Then Pauline's bottom will have burned in vain. She will not suffer for it much, I know. You'll be put out. I mean you so to be and may indeed arrange affairs to my own will on my return.

Alas, the cogitations that arise therefrom disturb me much. Pauline may run to her Mama. I think her capable of that. Perhaps you also do and rest your case to me thereon—a poacher who has set her traps in such a circle that there's no escape. Even so, the risk is worth the cause. If Pauline runs to her Mama then I shall have to cane you, too. *And* Phillipa. Would Agnes, though, allow—might beg forgiveness for you both and thus close all the doors to joy? I might persuade. It would not be the same. Agnes would stand beyond the door as once she did when Phillipa was strapped by me. The circle would repeat itself. Strapped . . . trapped . . . the words rebound on me.

Even so I prepare to ride—quite quietly and without your knowledge. A clink of cups announces preparations I would rather know not of. Agnes is vaguely somewhere, here or there. Such lust as was aroused in her was quick forgot. I resent that a little, yet it was as much an impediment as otherwise. "Women are unlikely after thirty-five," Papa would say. Mama laughed at him, said "Not always!" though she understood and—having him controlled—indulged his whims. Men of a certain age feel guilt with youth, yet satisfy themselves with it. Why not? I think too much, as Hannah said. "If you think about it all too much you will not do it," so she said.

The half-known is more attractive than the known, of course. Thus women who trail mystery are always sought. My steed's back ripples and disturbs my balls. How plump and round my daughter's bottom is! I must not think of that, must not, shall take to the four-acre field and ride across to view the smoke that rises from the distant town across the weald. There is movement there. I envisage the rooms, the closets, the commodes, the beds of pleasure rumpled up with lust, the unstirred dust upon the darkling stairs, the cries that waver in the night, the purses tight with unspent coins, shoes, boots thrown down and drawers a-droop—all merge and swirl within the far-off view.

Does Agnes wear her drawers or does she wait? Do you—does Phillipa? Are Pauline's off? At what moment of the emptying of the cups will Phillipa seize her wrists and draw her up to drag her squealing to the bed?

It were better that I had not known of this—but you intended that I should—intended that the images should dance, befuddle me and lure me there. I know you well enough. Perhaps you are Miss Atherton reborn, were never other than you meant to be, and I the victim of your sultry whims. I ride on fast, will not look back, will not. A hedge is taken clean—the grass afoot beneath my stallion's bounding hooves. . . . But wait! In vengeance, sensing I am gone, you may cane Pauline far too hard. I know you capable of that. Visions of hissing cane and hot-streaked cheeks. The twinkling of her dark, plump quim beneath, and Phillipa—victorious also now—astride upon her struggling back.

You bitch! I will not have it so! I turn and take the hedge again, horse snorting, whinnying, but landing well. I am as an unclipped Icarus come—will upset all your plans in my own wise, yet must invest my steps with caution. Out of sight of all the windows of the house I tether my horse and cut across a field that leads me in a winding way towards the garden and the summerhouse. Four-thirty. Have you started yet? I skirt dry bushes, come between the shrubs where Mabel stood and gazed at me hands clasped and dumb. The window, yes. I am repeating what I did before, but feel not wiser for it even so.

"NO-HO! What do you do! No, stop!"

The cry is much the same as was before, though Pauline's voice is shriller, more alert.

"Her dress off, Phillipa—and her chemise. I'll get her drawers down while you hold her so."

"You beasts! I'll tell on you! No! Not the cane! YEEE-AARGH!"

"Be quiet, you stupid thing—be quiet, or you'll get more than I intend. Hold tight her arms, Phillipa, quick!"

"No! AH! Oh save me someone—save me, do!"

I have not dared to look as yet, and as before fear that I might be seen. Excitement quickens in my loins. Go down, hot cock, go down—but it will not. Those thighs superb—that bottom round and full. I peep at last, most furtively I peep. Exactly as I envisaged, Phillipa is upon the shoulders of Pauline who, thrust face down upon the bed, already has her luscious bottom bared and with a single streak across its orb where you have coursed the cane across. Phillipa's knees are clenched against her sides and Pauline's face is hid beneath her cousin's weighty derriere.

"Can't get her dress off. Cane her as she is."

"NAR-HOOO! No, don't! NEEEE-YNNNNG! You cruel things, wicked girls, no—don't! FOOOO-EEEEEH!"

Twice more within my bleary sight the cane now skims that ardent orb, imprints it with its streaks of fire, makes Pauline's hips jerk, writhe and twist. "BOOO-HOOO!"

"What then did Papa do to you—then what? Come, speak the truth, Pauline, or else!"

"He . . . he . . . he put his. . . . OUCH! It burns!"

Another have you struck, and harder yet that causes me to wince and yet I view with heart-racing excitement all I see. Her quim's a fig that lures my eyes to it as much as does her wriggling orb. So luscious are the cheeks, full-blown, I fain would kiss and lick them—know my treachery in this, and yet must hear, must hear, so make myself excuse for this.

"You story, Pauline—oh, you fib!" SWEEEE-ISSSSH! HOOOO-WITTTT! the cane sings now again, brings me to grit my teeth as it sears in. "Now tell the truth, Pauline—come tell!"

"BLUB-BLUB-BLUB! He . . . he. . . . I m . . . m . . . made it up. He kissed me, though, and felt my. . . . YEEEK!"

"You felt *that* one, Miss, didn't you? How dare you say such—speak such naughty words, you awful story you, to tell such tales, and of our own Papa indeed."

"BOOO-HOOO! Oh, p . . . p . . . please don't do it more!"

SWEEE-ISSSSSH! SWEE-ISSH! HOO-WITTTTT! I feel them all and tense my buttocks to the searing strokes, balls swollen and my prick upthrust. Beneath the cloth, against the wall it rubs. The winking of Pauline's nether hole is seen as round about she squirms her fire-filled orb.

"You will not tell stories any more, Pauline?"

"I p . . . p . . . promise! No, I won't! Oh please!"

"And will in all respects obey?"

"O . . . b . . . b . . . bey? All right, I will, I will!"

"Well, we shall see. Get off her, Phillipa, and you Pauline, hold up your dress and face the window now."

"Oh, *why*? I can't stand still, I can't, I can't. NAH-HAAAAR! Elizabeth, please don't!"

"I will again, Miss, if you don't obey! Come to your posture—stand with legs apart as well I tell you to."

My god, you know! You know I look! Furtive as a beggar at a feast I dart away though scarce before a trembling Pauline turns, exquisite stockinged legs revealed, her belly white, her bush thrust forth to me. You bitch, you make me tremble with your tricks and laugh within yourself no doubt—I who dare not be seen, discovered here. Nor can I enter—rage—for you will tell Pauline that I have sneaked upon her thus, a mendicant of lust who dares not view more openly. A hugger-mugger now that I've become—been made by you—I ludicrously bend beneath the window, step away, and stand—yes—trembling at your trick, forlorn in my own garden, quite absurd.

"Elizabeth, don't make me stand thus, please! My bottom, oh it hurts, it does!"

The voices reach me still, at least. I will not move away, will not. Indeed cannot. I am as rooted here.

"Turn slowly, Pauline. Hold your dress up still! Walk slowly to the bed and kneel upon it with your bottom well thrust up." SWEEEE-ISSSSSH!

"YA-HOOOOO! You p . . . p . . . promised not to! Don't!"

"I promise nothing, Pauline. Do it now!"

"I'll t . . . t . . . tell Mama!"

"You won't. You have good reason not to, have you not?"

"D . . . d . . . don't know what you mean! Oh-ho! No, please don't cane me any more!"

"I won't, Miss, if you but obey. Well up now, legs apart, head down. No—do not hold her, Phillipa. She'll learn. Or else she'll get the cane once more."

"BOOOOO-HOOO! What do you do? Oh, take it OUT!"

"Be QUIET, Miss! It is not as big as Papa's prick but still will serve you well. Come, move your hips a little— surge them back and forth as you have learned to do. Last night perhaps?"

"Wh . . . wh. . . . WH . . . AAAART! Goo-HOOOO! Oh, not so much!"

"'Tis but a third or less of a stiff cock. And well you know that, I believe. Phillipa, sit beside her, tickle up her quim, your hand beneath her belly. Is she moist?"

"Delicious, darling—*really*, you should feel!"

"I may in due course, with my tongue. Her bottom's tight enough and sucks in well. Yes, bring her on, my love, yes—bring her on."

"WHOOOO-WHOOOO! It's w . . . w . . . wicked! Oh, my bottom stings!"

"And will do more in future, dear, if you still disobey. Will you not move to my thumb and surge your hips or must I cane you once again?"

"HA-HOOOO! I'll try. You c . . . c . . . caned me much too hard—you did!"

"A softer spurring did you have of Papa's birch no doubt, my sweet."

"You knew, you *knew*! Oh, horrid thing, you. . . . OOOOOH!"

Dear god, the world's upturned and all about! The bushes stare at me—the summerhouse is vibrant with the noise within. I, outcast, stand—a man without a ticket to the ball, one cheated, put upon, denied. There is but one thing now to do—regain my horse and ride away. I shall pretend I neither saw nor heard. You only guessed me at the window—*that* was it! I shall throw dust upon my clothes and have a tired, indifferent visage on return, shall linger in the town and come back late.

"Ah-hah! She's sprinkling now, Elizabeth!"

"DOO-DOO-DOO-DOOOO! You make it do it—OH!"

I stumble, fret my feet uncertain in the grass, then steal away. My head is buzzing with duplicities. A story first put up and then denied, and then found true!

You knew it to be true? Of course you did. That Luther is a devil after all—though no more so than I. A family party we shall have, perhaps. Or so I tell myself with irony. To what purpose did you cane Pauline except to taunt me yet again? The devil with it, I will have you out—sent back—and no more to be seen. You will in any event depart at Autumn's coming—Phillipa as well— no doubt then to receive the "softer spurring" of your Papa's birch. Oddly enough he will gain much from my ways with you who have, I imagine, a different temperament beneath his eye, are more modest and more sly, precisely as Pauline has been with me.

The town attracts. My goodness, I shall lead a different life—become a man who roams, has seen the Pyramids, is known in Paris at the best hotels, will visit India and see the Taj Mahal—returning bronzed, a houri on each arm. Yes—that will be the way of it henceforth. Regaining horse, I ride across the weald—would have it known that I am free and unemcumbered by you now, except that no one knows but you, which somehow irritates.

A little saddle-sore, not fit at all for sport, I reach the town, stable my horse at the Lord Wellington Hotel and make my way within and come with great surprise upon Grace Rutherford who is about to take her leave.

"You are staying here?"

"Dear Humphrey, what a great surprise! Why, no. I

came to make accommodation for a friend. Accommodation of a discreet sort, you understand. He will have a young friend with him—would have me, shall we say, instruct her just a little. Have you time to take a glass of wine?"

"Of course. I had the very question on my tongue! Besides that, you intrigue—must tell me more."

"Have I to tell *you*, or you me? I have sadly missed our young and pretty friend. Came you to a nice conclusion with her then?"

"Several, my dear, and all much to your taste. Waiter! A bottle of Chablis, if you will."

"Tell me all, Humphrey. I am agog. She is a pert one, that—had not the simple innocence I wished. I mind that she surprised you just a little, did she not?"

"'Twas but a test." My tone is bland, but slightly edged. Her eyes are quizzical, search deep my own as we take a corner table in the lounge, slim mirrors all about, the chairs red plush. Decidedly an air of comfort here. I must beware of this. Comfort makes confessors of us all.

"Not one well taken, though, by her. Have you had her bottom yet?"

Lines at the corners of her eyes, though not displeasing. I remember how her lips sucked so luxuriously upon my cock. There is a slight vulgarity about her that both intrigues and repels.

"She has taken to the stem, of course."

My answer makes her laugh, but then the waiter comes, distracts, fills up our glasses and retires, a look of utter boredom on his face. Dry as my saddle must his dull life be.

"How quaintly you put it, Humphrey! Even so, the phrase is nice. I may remember it for future use. As roses often have a good straight stem, the simile comes well. Provided you have watered well her rose, I mean."

"Of course. But tell me of your . . ."

"Is she your daughter, or your niece? I always like to know."

"Related distantly. It matters not." I drink too quickly, cannot meet her eyes. An emptiness falls on me like a pall. Better I had not met her. Better even I had not met you whose eyes can follow me through space and time.

"You are not happy, my dear. You should have let me help. I have a certain expertise in things, enjoy to watch, to coddle, coax. . . ."

"I know you do. Good heavens, Grace, you think me not accomplished in such things?" My irritation is my guilt, of course. She senses it, which helps me not, but is too clever with her smile. Hannah smiled thus and pushed my hand away from underneath her skirts. Superior. Am I to be the only one who's not? With an air of gaucheness that my irritation breeds, I glance towards the foyer and spring up. "Forgive me, Grace—someone whom I must see." Before she can reply I stride away and like an escaping felon reach the street and make towards my waiting horse.

The devil with all women such as she. I need them not.

The cane my conqueror shall be.

CHAPTER
twenty-three

Im have put myself, as I perceive, in a disadvantage, in a way. By adopting a calm silence on my return—which is as though to say that I know nothing of the summer-house events—I leave the field for you to take. Or it may be, of course, that Pauline will seek reprise with me as to her bottom's burnishing, but this I doubt. An air of quiet is in your eyes which I do not enjoy at all. If you saw me at the window, really saw. . . .

"Will you to town tomorrow with me, Humphrey? The girls are idle, will not come."

"My dear, I cannot, for I have to meet with Rutherford."

A grave mistake. I see your eyebrows rise, a smile quick as a ripple on your lips.

"A pity. What a pity—still. . . . You mean to have the village girls here soon?"

The question's artless, I am sure. All eyes upon me. I stir in my seat, wait with a tense annoyance for your nod that does not come. You smile again, look down and smooth your dress.

"The village girls, eh, what? I had forgotten it. A

226

matter of the clothes—oh, yes. Pauline had best take that in hand now that she's back. You have explained it to her?"

"Yes, Papa, I know of it. Elizabeth has told me of it."

"Quite. I'm sure that with your cousins you'll arrange it very well."

"They will indeed." The beam of Agnes twinkles all around. Blessed is she who thinks that lust is flown, that Pauline's re-arrival makes a pudding of my mind. And as to yours, you think to keep me out of it, no doubt—I who have tutored you to such a point, spent money on Miss Atherton. I rage within, but somehow keep my calm, excuse myself and then retire upstairs. It began here, did it not—on your return—in this quiet study when your drawers came down and flushed and bubbling came you to my lips.

The door opens after half an hour when I have picked up books galore and all put down unread. You come as quietly as you ever did. Idly you step towards my desk and trace your finger on the edge's rim.

"It will be better now, you know, with Pauline here."

"With Pauline? What? I do not understand."

"I thought you might, but then thought you might not. I caned her hard this afternoon. Were you not there?"

"I was not, no." My voice abrupt I turn away, finger the dust upon the sill and mindlessly take in the silent view. Where the trees stand, have ever stood, will stand. I tremble inwardly. You know I do. Hatred is love. I hate you now.

"It will be better because, well . . . if she did not know . . . ."

"If she did not . . . ?"

"If she came betwixt, between. You know well what I mean." Your hand slips into mine. You rest your arm against my head. I do not stir—should be outraged by what you now intend.

"You will have a good time of it, I have no doubt."

By introducing Pauline I perceive that you have blocked my way completely now. Your confidence is far too great, besides. You feel my anger surely in my mode of stillness. I do not respond to your small thumb that rubs against my own. How little must it have felt in Pauline's . . . no . . . I should not think of that.

"I'm sure we shall—and so will you!"

Your laughter tinkles and I turn about face set, eyes glowering, make to push your hand away, but cannot quite. To my alarm I touch your fingertips and feel an innocence of smoothness there.

"You know I cannot now, Elizabeth. Not with Pauline here, and. . . ."

"Oh, don't be silly. Had you but been there. . . . This afternoon, I mean."

At least I have this victory. You do not know.

"I was not. Shall I ask her? Would that put a blot upon your plans?"

"How angry you are with me! Do you not see that it was for the best? She offered up her bottom wonderfully. Well . . . afterwards she did." You giggle, reach up, kiss my lips. I cannot help myself, enfold your waist and feel the darling bulbing of your breasts against my shirt, the nipples hard and arrogant with youth. Excitement, too, perhaps, that stirs my loins, causes my knob to tingle, swell. Your eyes crease up with pleasure and your hand steals down to roll it lovingly the while I groan.

"Do not, Elizabeth! Don't taunt me so. If you have caned Pauline she will tell all, and all will be undone. So far from bettering matters. . . ."

"SHUSH! You do not listen to a word I say! I gave her a full dozen—nearly so. She writhed, sobbed, wriggled—all that one expects while held by Phillipa. You see, I tell you true. But I was held myself at first. One has to be—and then one slowly learns. My goodness, if you had but seen her bottom ripe and glowing! Then I made her stand, skirt up and legs apart, displayed, just as Miss. . . ."

"Miss Atherton, yes, I'm sure. My love, with you it's different—and with Phillipa, but with Pauline there I. . . ."

"What? With Pauline there you'll not intrude your cock? I know you will. Papa did birch her—I confess—but in my way I had to bring it out of her, just as he put his in her—oh!"

"You witch!" I cannot help myself. "You knew it all along, I swear you did."

"Perhaps."

We shuffle, sway, in love are locked—or locked in lust, it does not matter now. Upraised your skirts, my prick free in your hand. Liquid the darting of your pointed tongue as to the desk we move and with a sound that's petulant and sweet you bend to me, displaying free the tight cleft of your orb.

"You want to?"

"Yes—you know I do. Put it in slowly—hold my cheeks apart. AH-OOOH!" Back dipped, your tight and ardent globe receives the deep in-probing of my prick while from our lips there seep our wondering moans and little puffs as inch by inch it sheathes until my balls hang down beneath your curl-kissed nest.

And all is still and all is still.

"Undo my corsage. Slip your hand within and feel my tits. Don't move it yet—don't move it—ooooh!"

Wondrous your polished globes, gelatinous but firm, the silky skin that lures my fingers all about and feels the lustrous weight of all, tickling the lewd, upstarting tips.

"I w . . . w . . . will not need to cane you any more, my love."

"You will, indeed you will—sometimes—and Phillipa, and Pauline, too."

"Your aunt will be out tomorrow, dearest." Oozing out and pumping in. Oozing out and pumping in.

"Mmmmm . . . oh do it slowly, still. Finger my quim

and make me come. I'll cane them both tomorrow, lightly though, to make their bottoms tingle, offer up. I'll have them naked to their stockings stripped."

"They'll l . . . l . . . let you? Do you mean this true?"

"I do, I do! Of course they will—they must! They know the way of things—the way I am. St . . . st . . . stay quiet within your room at first, but listen and you'll hear. I'll leave the bedroom d . . . d . . . door unlocked. G . . . g . . . go faster! Oh! And when the c . . . c . . . cane has ceased to swish, come naked to your sh . . . sh . . . shirt, prick stiff and g . . . g . . . give it first to dear Pauline, she needs it now, right up her bottom . . . ooooooooh!"

"Elizabeth! . . . I'm coming! . . . Oh my love . . .!"

THE VICTORIAN LIBRARY

- [ ] *The Amorous Memoirs of Capt. Charles De Vane /* 62421-1 / $3.95
- [ ] *Astrid Cane* / 62461-0 / $3.95
- [ ] *Arabella* / 62478-5 / $3.95
- [ ] *Beatrice* / 17973-0 / $3.95
- [ ] *Birch in the Boudoir* / 62448-3 / $4.50
- [ ] *The Boudoir* / 17781-9 / $3.95
- [ ] *Caroline* / 62377-0 / $3.95
- [ ] *Clara Birch* / 62033-X / $3.95
- [ ] *Davina, or The Romance of Mesmerism* / 62452-1 / $3.95
- [ ] *Days at Florville* / 62482-3 / $3.95
- [ ] *Elizabeth* / 62037-2 / $3.95
- [ ] *Eveline* / 17892-0 / $3.95
- [ ] *Eveline II* / 17972-2 / $3.50
- [ ] *"Frank" and I* / 17751-7 / $3.95
- [ ] *The Gardens of the Night* / 62360-6 / $3.95
- [ ] *Jennie* / 62239-1 / $3.95
- [ ] *Julie* / 62240-5 / $3.95
- [ ] *Lady Beth* / 62328-2 / $3.95
- [ ] *Laura* / 62481-5 / $3.95
- [ ] *A Man with a Maid* / 17479-8 / $4.50
- [ ] *A Man with a Maid: Book II* / 17091-1 / $3.95
- [ ] *A Man with a Maid: Book III* / 17993-5 / $3.95
- [ ] *Maude Cameron and Her Guardian* / 62004-6 / $3.95
- [ ] *Miriam* / 62225-1 / $3.95
- [ ] *My Life and Loves* / 17124-1 / $4.95
- [ ] *My Secret Life* / 17397-X / $4.95
- [ ] *Natasha* / 62378-9 / $3.95
- [ ] *Nights of the Rajah* / 62027-5 / $3.95
- [ ] *Oh Wicked Country!* / 62447-5 / $3.25
- [ ] *Pleasure Bound: Three Erotic Novels* / 17977-3 / $4.95
- [ ] *Romance of Lust* / 17540-9 / $4.95
- [ ] *School for Scandal* / 62057-7 / $3.95
- [ ] *Secret Talents* / 62483-1 / $3.95
- [ ] *Suburban Souls* / 17541-7 / $4.95
- [ ] *Venus in the Country* / 62420-3 / $3.95
- [ ] *Venus School Mistress* / 62158-1 / $3.95